Presented to

_____

From

_____

On the Occasion of

_____

Date

_____

DAILY WISDOM

from the

BIBLE

Encouragement for Every Day

DAN & NANCY DICK

EDITED BY TRUDIE MARTINEAU

BARBOUR

© 1986 by Barbour Publishing, Inc.

Compiled by Connie Troyer.

ISBN 1-59310-367-0

All Scripture quotations are taken from the King James Version of the Bible.

Cover image © Getty Images, by Ed Collacott

Design: UDG | DesignWorks—cover, Charles Brock; interior, Robin Black

Published by Barbour Publishing, Inc., P.O. Box 719, Uhrichsville, Ohio 44683, www.barbourbooks.com

Our mission is to publish and distribute inspirational products offering exceptional value and biblical encouragement to the masses.

 Member of the
Evangelical Christian
Publishers Association

Printed in China.
5 4 3 2 1

Incline thine ear unto wisdom, and apply thine heart to understanding. . . . Then shalt thou understand the fear of the Lord, and find the knowledge of God.

PROVERBS 2:2, 5

Spiritual Growth

The proverbs of Solomon the son of David,
king of Israel; to give subtilty to the simple, to the
young man knowledge and discretion.

Proverbs 1:1, 4

The saying is certainly true which says, "Experience is the best teacher." It is through day to day living that we come to understand life. What we did not understand as children we come to know as adults. When we start upon a new endeavor we learn slowly, gathering more information and experience until we finally master it.

Our Christian life is like that. We start out inexperienced and with little knowledge, but then we grow in our understanding and commitment. Christ Himself spent a good deal of His life preparing for His ministry and work. Like Him, we are growing, maturing, and preparing for the Kingdom of God, which awaits us. When we search for God in the Bible and through prayer we are being made ready for our heavenly home. In this life, we never really arrive at "being" Christian, but we are ever "becoming" Christian. As long as we continue to learn, we continue to grow. In that growth lies wisdom.

Dear heavenly Father, grant that I might continue to learn more about You each and every day. Create in me a real hunger for Your truth. Amen.

An Awesome Power

The fear of the LORD is the beginning of knowledge:
but fools despise wisdom and instruction.

PROVERBS 1:7

Standing on the shore of a great ocean, one is amazed at the force of the waves crashing on the rocks. The vast expanse of water is awe-inspiring, and yet it is beautiful. Only a very foolish person would ignore the dangers presented by the sea, and yet, only a fool would not be attracted by its beauty. The ocean is to be feared and respected, but it is also to be experienced. Despite our sense of awe, or perhaps because of it, we are drawn to the water, to be immersed in it, to become part of it. Our true enjoyment of the surf comes when we enter in, but only when we understand its power.

The same is true of God. We stand in awe before Him, wisely cautious in the face of His power, and yet we long to know Him, to be united with Him. The wise pursue Him with all their heart, while the foolish ignore Him or reject Him through their fear. Once we understand the power of our Lord, this fear enables us to be with Him, immersed in Him, but always respecting His might.

O Lord, help me to know fear in a positive way, and set my feet on the path to wisdom. Amen.

Testing

But ye have set at nought all my counsel, and would none of my reproof: I also will laugh at your calamity; I will mock when your fear cometh.

PROVERBS 1:25–26

Once, when I was young, I climbed a tree against the wishes of my mother. I got high up in the branches and found that I could neither continue forward nor go back. I held tight to a large branch and began to cry. I yelled for my mother, and I could see her walk out to where I was captive. Instead of being angry, as I thought she would be, she began to laugh, and placing her hands on her hips, she said, "I told you not to try to climb up there. Now look at you. Why do you think I tell you not to do some things?"

All too often, our inclination is to test God. We know what He says He wants us to do, but we do other things instead. We try to get away with things we know we should not. When we find ourselves in trouble we look to God to bail us out, and we cannot understand why He doesn't jump to our aid. Often God allows us to struggle through adversity in order to learn that He means what He says.

Dear heavenly Father, I so often do what I know You do not want me to. Forgive my foolishness and disobedience. Help me to heed Your will, not my own. Amen.

TRUE WEALTH

My son, if thou wilt receive my words,
and hide my commandments with thee; so that thou
incline thine ear unto wisdom, and apply
thine heart to understanding; yea, if thou criest after
knowledge, and liftest up thy voice for
understanding; if thou seekest her as silver,
and searchest for her as for hid treasures; then shalt
thou understand the fear of the LORD,
and find the knowledge of God.

PROVERBS 2:1–5

Following Christ requires our all. In order for us to walk in His footsteps we must be totally dedicated: body, mind, and soul. We need to listen carefully to the word of God, and we must learn to apply it. We should spend time in contemplation using our minds to gain a deeper understanding of God's will. We should open our hearts in order to feel God's presence in our lives. We should praise God with our voices and shout His glories. We should talk with other believers and share our questions and experiences.

We devote such great energies to the acquisition of material goods. Wealth is so appealing. Yet, we fail to understand that true wealth comes only through a relationship with God. The knowledge of God is worth more than the finest riches. God desires that we pursue Him with the same devotion that we pursue material gain. Let that be our aim.

Lord God, no matter what I own, what I might possess, without You I have nothing. Turn my sight from this world, dear God, and help me to seek only You—body, mind, and soul. Amen.

TIME TOGETHER

Then shalt thou understand righteousness,
and judgment, and equity; yea, every good path.

PROVERBS 2:9

Jesus Christ selected for himself a band of twelve rough, rugged men to be His disciples. These men knew very little of qualities like gentleness, compassion, kindness, and giving. Prior to Jesus' coming to them they had very little reason to consider any of these traits. Their paths were many, but none would have been considered good. None until Christ came along.

During their three years with Jesus, the disciples learned everything there was to know of these qualities. They came to understand all that Jesus tried to show them. They carried these qualities of goodness into the world and taught others to follow them.

If we will take time to spend with Christ through prayer, Bible reading, and devotion, we too will learn these traits. We will learn to follow the good paths that Jesus followed. This is what it means to be a Christian. The key is in spending time with God in order to learn them.

Remind me, heavenly Father, that I should spend time with You today and every day. Make me a disciple of Yours, anxious to learn all that You would teach me. Amen.

QUESTIONING BELIEFS

[For God will] deliver thee from the strange woman,
even from the stranger which flattereth
with her words; which forsaketh the guide of her youth,
and forgetteth the covenant of her God.

PROVERBS 2:16–17

Society has come up with some wonderful philosophies over the years. "If it feels good, do it," "I'm okay, you're okay," "God is dead." Every year there is some new easy belief to buy into. Good, solid beliefs are hard to come by, and they are even harder to hold onto. Someone is always trying to give us something new to believe in.

It's good to know that God is watching over us and that He is there for us when we turn to

Him with our doubts and questions. Prayer is the direct connection that we have with God. When we find ourselves faced with new and different beliefs, it is a good idea to take them to God. He will provide the light we need to closely scrutinize different beliefs. Jesus said, "I am the way, the truth, and the life: no man cometh unto the Father, but by me" (John 14:6). If we will remain committed to our Christian faith, God will help us to see the folly of believing in the easy philosophies offered to us by society. God wants us to come to believe in Him with as few doubts as possible. He will always help us to learn as much as we can when our Christian faith is challenged.

God, I think that I know what to believe, but new things come up almost every day. Help me to sort out what is right and good to believe, and what is not. Grant me Your wisdom. Amen.

PRIZED POSSESSIONS

For the upright shall dwell in the land,
and the perfect shall remain in it.

PROVERBS 2:21

My grandmother had a special cedar box that she kept all of her prized possessions in. I used to sit with her at the kitchen table as she would unwrap her treasures. There were old pictures, coins, gems, a lock of hair, a ribbon from a long passed contest, a pair of old glasses, a hand carved spinning top, and a dozen other knick-knacks. My grandmother would tell the story of each and every one, and the love and affection she shared with those memories will stay with me all of my life.

I think God is a little like that. We are His treasures, and He has set aside a special place for us. Each of us brings forth a feeling of love and affection from God, and He cherishes each one of us. We are each one precious in the good Lord's sight, and He knows our individual stories by heart. It is good to know that God loves us so much that He will keep us for all time in a very special place that He has made especially for us. The future glory that awaits all Christian believers is beyond our wildest imagination, and yet we can rest assured that it will far outshine anything we have yet experienced.

Thank You, Lord, that I am one of Your prized possessions. Keep me ever in Your care, and cover me with Your divine love and affection. I praise You for Your love, and I will try to be a fond remembrance in Your heart. Amen.

PLEASING OTHERS

Be not wise in thine own eyes: fear the LORD,
and depart from evil. It shall be health to thy navel,
and marrow to thy bones.

PROVERBS 3:7−8

A law student looked for honors and approval
from his professors and his peers. His
motivation was to "look good" in all that he did.
He pursued unbelievably high standards, and when
he eventually failed, he was crushed. All of his work
to come out on top provided him with nothing.
He left law school feeling cheated, a failure.

It is easy to fall into a trap of trying to live up
to society's standards. We try to look good for
other people. We play at popularity games and try
to impress others with our position and prestige.
This is sad, because who we should really be
trying to please is God. He has created each of us
with special gifts and talents, and it is His will that
we do nothing more than live up to the potential
He created for us. We don't have to try to be

something we're not with God. He knows us better than we know ourselves. What is important for us to do is find out who we really are and try to remain true to that identity. God loves us just as we are, and as long as we believe that God knows what He is doing, then we can be satisfied with ourselves as He created us.

Lord, help me to realize my potential. Make me less a person-pleaser and more a God-pleaser. Grant that I might discover my gifts and talents, then assist me to use them as You would have them used. Amen.

God's Many Miracles

The LORD by wisdom hath founded the earth;
by understanding hath he established the heavens.
By his knowledge the depths are broken up,
and the clouds drop down the dew.

PROVERBS 3:19-20

The word "miracle" sounds strange in this day and age. We have become too sophisticated to accept miracles anymore. It is sad that we have lost such a wonderful idea. A miracle used to be an event which was beyond simple explanation and understanding. Many people say that miracles don't happen anymore, if they ever did.

If only people would open their hearts and begin looking more deeply than they are able with their eyes alone. When we see a beautiful sunset, it affects more than just our eyes. When we ponder the wonder of human life at birth, we are experiencing much more than a mere sensory event. The nighttime sky, the pounding surf of the ocean, the laughter of a child—all of these are miracles in a sense, and all of them are evidence of the wonder of God. It is a special joy to see the world with eyes open to miracles, and to feel life with a heart attuned to God's love. If we understand God, then we must believe in His miracles.

Make me a believer, Lord. Show me the multitude of miracles You have created and are creating. Let me understand creation the way You intended it. Amen.

HEALING

My son, let them not depart from thine eyes:
keep sound wisdom and discretion: When thou liest down,
thou shalt not be afraid: yea, thou shalt lie down, and
thy sleep shall be sweet.

PROVERBS 3:21, 24

A doctor had been practicing medicine for a number of years when he found that he couldn't sleep at night. After a long successful career, the doctor suddenly felt that his work was futile and senseless. As hard as he tried, he could not save everyone he treated. Many of the people he treated never got any better. His early dreams of healing those who were in pain and suffered began to fail. Night after night he tossed and turned, struggling to make peace with what he felt was failure.

An understanding of God and what God wants from us as his children can help us to have calm nights. No human being can take responsibility for life and death. God gave life, and He is the ruler of all life. For some people, God has chosen to allow them to assist in the healing process. He has given

men and women the minds and talents to save and
sustain life, yet it is always God who ultimately
makes the decision of who will live and who will
die. Our responsibility is to use our gifts and
talents to the best of our abilities. If we will try to
do so, we can count on God's richest blessing.

*Help me, Father, to utilize the wonderful gifts and
graces that You have seen fit to grant me. Bless me as
I attempt to be the best person I can be, the person
You made me to be. Amen.*

GOOD REWARDS

Be not afraid of sudden fear, neither of the desolation of the wicked, when it cometh. For the LORD shall be thy confidence, and shall keep thy foot from being taken.

PROVERBS 3:25–26

A teacher returned to her classroom to find chaos had broken out. Paper, pencils, and erasers were flying through the air, pictures were drawn on the blackboards and walls, children were running all around the room, and the noise was deafening. One little girl sat quietly

in the back corner, refusing to enter into the mischief. As the teacher began to scold the class, she remembered the little girl who was well-behaved. After class, she pulled the young child aside and told her how much it meant to her that she had remained silent and obedient.

Often we feel as though our good acts are missed. When we don't receive credit and acclaim, we feel cheated. What we need to remember is that none of our actions go unnoticed by God. He sees our every move, and he applauds us when we refuse to do those things that we know we should not but that our society seems to approve of. Our reward will never come from this life but from the life that awaits us with our heavenly Father. His blessing is ever with us if we will only be patient and believe.

Father, often I feel as though my good behavior is ignored or forgotten. Forgive me for being prideful, and help me to know that You see me at both my best and worst and love me all the time. Amen.

The Freedom of Choice

Hear, O my son, and receive my sayings; and the years of thy life shall be many. I have taught thee in the way of wisdom; I have led thee in right paths.

Proverbs 4:10–11

Many times I have heard parents lament, "What have I done wrong?" Parents are all too willing to take the blame when their children make poor choices or get themselves into trouble. Parents want so much for their children to succeed and have pleasant, carefree lives. That is why there is special joy in seeing children succeed. Mothers

and fathers can feel pride and take some credit for their children when they do well. It is an honor to the parents of children who succeed, that they have done a good job of bringing them up. When parents take interest in their children and treat them with respect and care, they are giving them as great a gift as is possible. Those children who come from these types of families are supposed to have the greatest chance of living good lives when they are grown.

Our heavenly Father has tried to instruct us in the ways that lead to eternal life. He has allowed us to make our own choices, though, and we must take responsibility for them, bad or good. It is His greatest wish that we follow the wisdom of His will. When we do so, it is to His glory as well as ours, that we have learned well. By listening to our heavenly Father, our lives are enriched and the years of our lives will be multiplied.

O God, You have been such a loving Father. Forgive me that I have often ignored the instructions You have given me for my sake. Help me to follow Your will and remain steadfast in my commitment to You. Amen.

THE LURE OF SIN

Enter not into the path of the wicked,
and go not in the way of evil men. Avoid it, pass not
by it, turn from it, and pass away.

PROVERBS 4:14–15

There are plants in nature which are lovely
to look at, but they are deadly. There are
animals which seem harmless and even attractive
but are dangerous. In life there are many things
which seem appealing; they have hidden traps.
Sin is a lot like that. Most sins are attractive and
tempting. We find ourselves desiring things which
could possibly harm us. Often we are lured by
things which we know will hurt us, but we want
them badly enough to take the risk.

It doesn't make sense that we would do things
which we know will harm us. The wages of sin
is death, and yet it seems that we pursue sin
believing that its wages are the finest reward we
could possibly attain. A wise person avoids life
threatening situations at any cost. That is what we
should do as Christians. We should do everything
in our power to avoid sin, which should be as

odious to us as death itself. It is not enough to try not to sin, but we should do anything in our power to avoid it, turn from it, move as far away from it as possible, and leave it as far behind as can be. It is by a conscious effort that we avoid sin, just as it is by choice that we do good.

May I choose the right path, Almighty God, turning from what I know You would not have me do in order to pursue what is fitting in Your sight. Guide me through the power of Your Holy Spirit. Amen.

SHINING YOUR LIGHT

But the path of the just is as the shining light,
that shineth more and more unto the perfect day.

PROVERBS 4:18

A young woman worked at a factory which was about ten blocks from where she lived. She could walk to work, but to do so she had to cross a railroad bridge which was treacherous going when the sun began to set. During the winter months it was doubly dangerous due to slippery conditions as well as darkness. The woman would have avoided the crossing altogether had it not been for the crossing guard. Each evening as the woman approached the crossing, the guard waved a lantern to signal that he awaited. Using the powerful light, he would lead the woman by the hand across the bridge. Throughout her life

the woman never forgot the kindness and help of the older crossing guard.

The lives of those people who are touched by the love of Christ are like guiding lights to others who have yet to find Christ in their lives. They can provide guidance and help, and they shine forth as bright examples of how good life can be. God's light can shine through us if we will only let it. We have the opportunity to show others the difference that Christ can make. When we live life empowered by the light of God, we live as He wishes we would.

Father, please make me a light for my world. Let me shine forth with Your goodness, care, and love. Let all who look to me see Your grace. Help me to reflect the saving light of Christ which You have lovingly given me. Amen.

The Straight Path

Let thine eyes look right on,
and let thine eyelids look straight before thee.

PROVERBS 4:25

When I was in high school I was quite a runner. Day after day I would train, running seventeen miles in the morning and seventeen miles at night. I ate all of the proper foods, took good care of myself, got plenty of rest, and I followed the instructions of my coaches. One of the most important instructions they ever gave me was: When you're in the race, keep your head straight and look forward. Never turn your head. If you do, you'll break your stride, and it could cost you the race. I saw it happen time and time again. Runners would just cast a quick glance over their shoulder to see where the other runners were, and that was all it took. They would stumble, lose concentration, and the other runners would catch up and pass.

The rule is one that we should, as Christians, learn to follow. As long as we keep our eyes on Jesus, we will do fine. It is when we are distracted, when we lose sight of God in our lives that we get ourselves into trouble. The rule is a simple one, but an important one: Let thine eyes look right on. . . right on Jesus Christ our Lord.

Keep my sight straight, Almighty God. Let me see only You in my life. Make me aware of Your presence every day, and never let me turn my eyes from You. Be the vision of my life. Amen.

A Watchful Eye

*Hear me now therefore, O ye children, and depart
not from the words of my mouth. Lest thou give thine
honor unto others, and thy years unto the cruel.*

PROVERBS 5:7, 9

Whether we know it or not, we are being
watched. Whenever we claim to be
something, people will watch us to see whether or
not we live up to our claims. Athletes are judged
by their performances. Investors are valued for
their ability to make big money. Policemen are
judged by their abilities to perform well under
fire. What is it that Christians are judged for?

When we call ourselves Christians we are
claiming to be mirror images of Christ for all the
world to see. We are presenting ourselves as
examples of what God had in mind when he put
men and women on this earth. It is a presumptuous
claim we make, and one that carries with it a great
amount of responsibility. One of the greatest sins
we can ever commit is to call ourselves Christians

then act in ways which are unacceptable in the sight of the Lord. We must continually study the word of God and follow all of the instructions that God has given to us. We must devote ourselves to imitating Christ in all ways possible. When we fail to do so, we bring dishonor not only on ourselves but also on the entire Christian church.

I pray that I might learn to walk carefully in the steps of Jesus Christ, Almighty Father. Grant that I might be an honor to Your truth in all ways. Be with me to shine Your light through my life that others may see Your greatness. Amen.

REAL LOVE

*Let thy fountain be blessed: and rejoice with the
wife of thy youth. Let her be as the loving hind and
pleasant roe; let her breasts satisfy thee at all times;
and be thou ravished always with her love.*

PROVERBS 5:18–19

While walking along the beach one evening,
I saw an elderly couple strolling on the
boardwalk. The man was blind, and his wife was
lovingly leading him along. Her hands were
gnarled with arthritis, and her legs were swollen.
Both people looked as though they had lived
difficult lives. Despite this, I could see the love
with which the woman looked upon her mate.
I walked up to the couple and told them that I was
struck with how much in love they looked. The
woman appeared a little embarrassed, but her
husband spoke right up and said, "We've been
married fifty-two years. I could never have made
it without her. When everything else goes bad,
I know I've still got the best little woman in the
world to love me."

That old gentleman knew the real secret of happiness. It is never in the things we have or don't have. It's not in what happens to us or doesn't happen. The best thing in life is love. Those who are lucky enough to find someone to share their lives with enjoy a special gift from God. But for every person, the love of God is very real, and very much freely given. We can be happy because we can know we are loved. Praise God.

O Lord, giver of life and giver of love, though I am unworthy, I thank You for loving me so much. Help me to know Your love at all times, and grant that I might be able to always spread that love wherever I might go. Amen.

The True Way

And why wilt thou, my son, be ravished with
a strange woman, and embrace the bosom of a stranger.

A young woman sobbed, "I just don't know what to believe anymore! I don't feel God with me like I used to." Her life had gone from bad to worse. She had followed in a long line of bad relationships and bad decisions. She had taken and lost a dozen jobs. She had moved from place to place and was swept up in every new fad to come along. She had joined a group of young people who gathered to meditate and chant together. It was the only place that she felt accepted, but even there she found little comfort as her life crumbled around her. Throughout her childhood she had been a member of a church, and now she felt that she was every bit as devoted with her new group. Still, it wasn't enough.

There is no substitute for the truth and saving power of Jesus Christ. Other groups and sects may appear to be sincere and good, but they are "strange women" who lure us from what is right and good to things we should avoid. The Lord has said clearly, "I am the way, the truth, and the life: no man cometh unto the Father, but by me" (John 14:6). Other paths may seem good, but they are false paths that lead nowhere. Stay close to God, avoid "strangers," and all will be well.

There is so much that looks good to me, Father. Protect me from the things which would lead me far from You. Steer me back to You when I stray. Guide my steps by Your loving light, Almighty God. Amen.

WITHIN THE MEANS

My son, if thou be surety for thy friend,
if thou has stricken thy hand with a stranger,
thou art snared with the words of thy mouth, thou art
taken with the words of thy mouth.

PROVERBS 6:1—2

The young couple was delighted when the first credit card came. They felt swept up in the power they had to purchase some of the things they'd always wanted, without having to part with a large sum all at once. One credit card followed another, and each one was used to its limit. New clothes, new furniture, appliances, stereos, vacations, gadgets—all swept in with seeming ease.

Then the bills came, and the ability to pay them was sorely lacking. The pressure to pay mounted, and it was followed by the frustration of losing all the nice things, then came the shame of recrimination and bad credit. What had seemed like a good deal in the beginning was nothing more than a nightmare in the end.

It is often easy to be snared by deals that seem to offer something for nothing. There is no such thing. Jesus told His disciples that they were to work for what they received and not to take any more than was needed. They were not to "strike deals" but let their "yes be yes, and their no be no." It is never wise to live beyond our means to the point where we become a slave to our transactions. In all ways, we should try to work with what God has given to us, waiting on the time when we may attain good things without going into debt.

Help me to avoid the traps which I find in my path each day, O Lord. Grant me the wisdom to know the difference between need and want and never sacrifice my integrity in order to obtain objects. Amen.

On the Alert

Yet a little sleep, a little slumber, a little folding of the hands to sleep: so shall thy poverty come as one that travelleth, and thy want as an armed man.

PROVERBS 6:10–11

The white lines flashed past hypnotically. The road stretched into an endless ribbon of gray. The sound of the radio faded in and out, and the car seemed to sweep the road with a mind of its own. The tires skidded in the soft gravel of the shoulder, and, had it not been for a sturdy guardrail, the car would have gone over the edge of a deep

ravine. By the time the foggy mist had lifted from my mind, I was sitting at an odd angle, counting my blessings for being still alive. I had dozed just briefly, perhaps not even a minute, but that was all the time it took for me to end in the ditch. It could have been all the time needed to end my life.

Sin is like that. It creeps up on us, makes us feel comfortable and lazy, and then it strikes when our defenses are down. The results can be tragic. Moral alertness is as important to our spiritual lives as physical alertness is to making sure we stay safe in an automobile. It is when we "fall asleep at the wheel" that evil can take its toll in our lives. The wise driver avoids the road when he or she is physically tired. Isn't it as wise for us, as Christians, to avoid those situations in our lives when we know we are not strong or when we are most susceptible?

Almighty God, I often grow drowsy in my spiritual pilgrimage. When I am in need of rest, be my stronghold. Protect me from the wiles of the evil one. Strengthen me that I might resist evil, so that it will flee from me. Amen.

The Abomination of Pride

These six things doth the LORD hate: yea, seven are
an abomination unto him: a proud look.

Proverbs 6:16–17

The new girl stepped cautiously into the classroom. She flinched as she looked at the people in the room. They were all dressed in the latest fashions, had nice hairstyles, and carried expensive purses and book bags. She looked down at her faded blue jeans and sneakers. A flush came to her cheeks. When she looked up, she saw that many of the girls and boys were looking at her with condescending sneers. She wished she could sink into the floor. Before she could control it, tears came into her eyes, and she turned away to avoid further embarrassment. Out of nowhere a voice came forth, "Hi, my name's Janet. What's yours?" Carefully, the young girl looked up to see a smiling, friendly face.

An attitude can be as damaging as an unkind word or a forceful blow. We wield great power in the way we treat other people. If we think that we are better than other people, it will show in our manner, our looks, our words, and our actions. God despises the proud and haughty attitudes that people develop. Our duty as Christians is to look at all individuals as equals, brothers and sisters whom we can reach out to. When we look down on others, we do not just withdraw our reach to them, but to Christ as well.

Dear Jesus, help me to see our spirit in all people I meet. Be sure that I never turn from another person due to pride or haughtiness. Teach me to love those around me as You would love them. Amen.

THE ABOMINATION OF LYING

These six things doth the LORD hate: yea, seven are an abomination unto him: a false witness that speaketh lies.

PROVERBS 6:16, 19

The little girl threw herself into a fit, thrashing around on the ground, spitting and ranting. The crowd stood around her in amazement. Wide-eyed the little girl pointed at a woman in the crowd, and immediately the magistrates took hold of her and whisked her off to prison. Thus go many stories of the Salem witch trials in America.

The fabrications of a few over-imaginative children took root and grew to monstrous proportions. Men and women lost their lives because of the lies of babes. A lie is the worst form of stealing a person can commit. It robs the victim of credibility and honor. It strikes silently and cruelly, and often it allows no room for

defense. When we lie, we display selfishness like no other.

Jesus said that He was the truth. If we want to get close to Christ, we must put lies and deceitfulness from our hearts. Our words must be kind and reflect the concern and care of Jesus Christ Himself. When we are honest, we take hold of the truth of Christ and spread it to others that we meet. When we lie, even a little bit, we deny the power of truth and reject the goodness that being honest brings. It is by living honest, straightforward lives that we move closer to God in all His glory.

I wish that I could be the person You want me to be, Almighty God. I find that I am dishonest, both with You and with myself. Empower me with a spirit of truth, that I might always live honestly and openly in Your sight. Amen.

KEEPING THE COMMANDMENTS

My son keep my words, and lay up my commandments
with thee. Keep my commandments, and live; and my law
as the apple of thine eye. Bind them upon thy fingers,
write them upon the table of thine heart.

PROVERBS 7:1–3

There was a man who spent all his days sitting
by an old firehouse telling stories to the
neighborhood children. The youngsters would flock
around the man to hear him tell of bygone days.
One striking feature of the old gentleman was that
around each of his fingers he had tied a different
colored string. The children would ask what the
strings were for, and the old man would say that
each one was to remind him of something
important. This was the way he remembered
things. But for everyone who came to him, he had
this to share.

"You don't need strings to remember the most
important things. God gave us ten fingers and ten
commandments, and if you keep one commandment
on each finger, then you'll never forget any of them."

The commandments of God should be as much a part of us as the fingers which are part of our hands. If we take care to remind ourselves of the laws of God, then they will be forever inscribed on the very "table" of our heart.

I continue to forget the things I should do. Help me to remember what You would have me do. I cannot hope to be the person You want me to be without Your help. Amen.

BEAUTIFUL SPEECH

Hear; for I will speak of excellent things;
and the opening of my lips shall be right things.

PROVERBS 8:6

There was a woman whom everyone dearly
loved. She never lacked for company,
because so many people flocked to spend time
with her. She had the ability to engage anyone,
old or young, male or female, black or white,
intelligent or simple, in delightful conversation.
With a beautiful voice she would tell stories of
bygone days and share dreams and wishes with
anyone who would listen. She was full of
compliments but never empty flattery. In every
situation, she knew the perfect thing to say.
In trouble, she spoke words that soothed, in times
of stress, she spoke words of comfort, and in good
times, she knew the perfect joke or anecdote
to share.

The gift of speech is a valuable one. It also carries with it great responsibility. We are commanded to avoid silly or coarse speech but to always use words to uplift and praise. Our words should reflect the presence of God in our hearts. Only the most excellent and right things should spring forth from our mouths.

Let the words of my mouth always produce what is pleasing in Your sight, O Lord. Let me build up, rather than tear down. May my speech reflect my great love for You. Amen.

Lord,
I want this prayer
imbedded in my heart.

A Heartfelt Desire

I love them that love me;
and those that seek me early shall find me.

PROVERBS 8:17

A young girl disappeared on her way home
from school. Her parents were in a panic,
and they called the police to help find her. After
two days of searching, the police put her in a file,
and the parents went away depressed. On their
own, they decided that they would do anything
necessary to find their little girl. They began a
search of their own. For six years they dedicated
themselves to the recovery of their only child.
After long years of desperately hoping and endlessly
searching, the pair found their daughter, living just
a few miles away with the woman who had
abducted her. Many times in the six years the couple
had wanted to give up. Repeatedly, they faced
feelings of futility and frustration. In spite of
impossible odds and lack of assistance, the pair
found their daughter and were reunited at long last.

When something is the desire of our heart,
it should possess us totally. How many of us

pursue God with the same diligence as the young couple pursued their daughter? God wants us to do so. Nothing pleases Him more than knowing that we love Him totally and completely. If we will seek God, with our whole being, His promise is that we will find Him.

Sometimes I lose patience when I wait for You to answer my prayers, O Lord. Give me the patience I so desperately need. Help me to pursue You in all ways at all times. Thank You for Your promise to always be there when I seek You. Amen.

KEEPING WATCH

*Blessed is the man that heareth me, watching daily
at my gates, waiting at the posts of my doors.*

PROVERBS 8:34

A security guard worked at the same job,
watching the gate of a chemical plant,
for fifteen years. For that entire time, no one had
ever tried to break into the plant. The guard
watched television, read books and magazines,
drank sodas, and walked the grounds. Often,
he would doze off, passing the long, tedious hours
in slumber. It hadn't always been that way. When
he was first hired, he had sat alertly at his post,
making his rounds promptly and completely.
He had spent hours working on ways to improve
security at the factory. That hadn't lasted long.
The dull routine of the work and the late hours
took their toll. As time passed, so did the
guard's enthusiasm.

One night, while the guard slept, three men
broke into the plant and made off with thousands
of dollars worth of valuable chemicals and drugs.

In an instant, the guard lost his position because of his inattention when it mattered most.

Christians need to take heed. Our attention must be on the Lord. We never know what might lie ahead, and so we should consciously try to be the best we can be in all circumstances. If we live each day as if it were the day we would meet our Maker, then we won't be embarrassed on the day it finally comes.

I pray that I might be alert and fully awake to my duties as Your loving disciple. As I follow Your will, let me not grow weary or tired, but fill me with every energy that I might be ready when my time comes. Amen.

The Royal Treatment

Wisdom hath builded her house, she hath hewn out her seven pillars: she hath killed her beasts; she hath mingled her wine; she hath also furnished her table.

PROVERBS 9:1−2

When I first began my ministry, I did so as a student in seminary. I had never served people officially before, and it surprised me when I was treated with so much respect and consideration. People showed that they had faith in me and it helped me to be able to minister to them—many

of whom were much older than I was. I was treated royally and was a little embarrassed because I didn't think I deserved it.

When we come into God's presence we may find ourselves surprised at how well God treats us. We come to Him as sinners, ashamed and afraid, and He treats us like kings and queens. We are not strangers who receive the lesser quality, but we are sons and daughters, welcomed home, and treated to only the best. God lays out the finest for His children, and it doesn't matter that we are undeserving. Children rarely deserve the love their parents have for them, but love, true love, cannot be earned. Love is a gift, and God freely gives His love to each and every child who will accept it. All we must do is accept the gift, not earn it. Wisdom comes to those who don't question the giver but accept the gift with gratitude.

Gracious and giving God, I cannot give You great enough thanks for all You offer to me, a humble child. Help me to give others some of the precious, unconditional love that You have given me. Amen.

THE FEAR OF THE LORD

The fear of the LORD is the beginning of wisdom:
and the knowledge of the holy is understanding.
For by me thy days shall be multiplied,
and the years of thy life shall be increased.
If thou be wise, thou shalt be wise for thyself: but if thou
scornest, thou alone shalt bear it.

PROVERBS 9:10–12

A young woman took a job at a zoo tending animals. Her third week on the job, she was shown how to feed the lions, tigers, and other big cats. Large portions of meat were stabbed by long spears, and then they were stuck through the bars of the cages to the animals. While in training, a piece of meat slipped from the end and lay half in and half out of the cage. The woman moved up and reached to pick up the meat. The lion inside the cage growled and pounced against the bars, reaching through and badly scratching the young woman. Her trainer rushed over and said, "Don't ever do that. Use the stick. If you had been closer and the cat's reach a little longer, you wouldn't be here now. I hope you remember that scratch the rest of your life."

In so many situations we feel that we are in control, that nothing can happen to us. We forget how truly fragile we are. We become complacent and lose our fear, our respect, for things we should remember about. The fear of the Lord is nothing more than knowing who He is and respecting Him. If we learn that fear, all our days will be long, and our lives will be safe and happy.

O Lord, help me to keep from letting down my guard for even one minute. Open my eyes to my limitations and grant that I might acknowledge my shortcomings. Only You are God, and I worship and praise You with all my heart. Amen.

DILIGENCE

He becometh poor that dealeth with a slack hand:
but the hand of the diligent maketh rich. He that
gathereth in summer is a wise son: but he that sleepeth
in harvest is a son that causeth shame.

PROVERBS 10:4–5

Two nurses were in the running for a staff position in a large metropolitan hospital. One was a hard working young woman from the Midwest who had striven her whole life to be the best nurse she could possibly be. She studied long

and hard and was at the top in her class.
She continued to study and learn new techniques
and practices. The other was a young man whose
father was the hospital administrator. He did his
job, but no more. He did just what had to be done,
and that was all. He figured he was the favorite as
far as the new position went, so he sat back and
awaited the decision. He was shocked when he
learned that the young woman had been selected.

There is nothing to be gained by resting on our
laurels. Hard work and integrity are important
values to possess. If we can learn to be disciplined
in our daily work, then we can improve our
spiritual discipline as well. It is pleasing to God
when we put forth our best efforts. When we
refuse to do our best, then we are failing to utilize
the talents and gifts that God has given to us all.

I want to be a faithful and devout servant, O Lord,
doing all that is required of me, using my talents in
the best possible way. Help me to do what is right,
keep me diligent, and turn me away from the
temptation to avoid my responsibilities. Amen.

DISHONESTY

He is in the way of life that keepeth instruction:
but he that refuseth reproof erreth.

<small>PROVERBS 10:17</small>

The judge watched carefully to see where his golfing partners were. Confident that he wasn't seen, he gave his ball a hefty kick. The ball traveled forward about twenty-five feet, onto a soft patch of close-cropped grass, in direct line with the green. He saw nothing wrong with it. He had done it as long as he golfed, and he told himself that his partners did it, too. On this occasion a booming voice cried out, "Hey, what are you trying to pull? Your ball was in the trees!" A raucous verbal battle ensued, with both sides

accusing the other side of cheating. Regardless of guilt, the judge always defended himself completely.

We really do kid ourselves when we think cheating is a way to get ahead. There is nothing to be gained by cheating. Our victories are empty ones, and we open ourselves to criticism and doubt. We lose our credibility and turn people against us. It is in honesty and truth that we find fulfillment. God dwells in truth, and He loves honesty. This is the way of life, but the way of death is through sin.

I am sorry for the ways that I try to get ahead by dishonesty. I am not honest with myself, and then I am not honest with You. Forgive my deceptions, and lead me in the light of Your truth, O God, now and forever. Amen.

MINDFUL WORDS

In the multitude of words there wanteth not sin:
but he that refraineth his lips is wise.

PROVERBS 10:19

The board meeting had dragged on and on. Every person seemed to have an opinion that they wanted to share. The chairperson had aired her views a number of times. She droned on and on about the point she was trying to make.

The rest of the staff were no different. A lot of words were spoken, but very little was being said. Then the program coordinator raised his hand and asked to be recognized. He had not said a word throughout the whole long discussion, but now he broke silence. He spoke slowly and deliberately, saying a few simple sentences, but he brought a hush over the entire room. He spoke the truth, and everyone saw the virtue of his argument immediately. That was the way he had always been.

It is a true gift to be able to listen and speak carefully. Too often we speak just to hear our own voices. People rarely get in trouble for saying too little; it is when they say too much that they feel regret. Jesus often sat and listened to the people. He let all sides speak their piece, then He would reply. His answers were direct, short, and to the point. People trusted Him because He said nothing more than what was needed. Would that we could learn to do likewise.

Please make me slow to speak, quick to listen, and grant me the wisdom to speak as Christ would. Fill my mouth with Your Holy Spirit. Amen.

STRENGTH IN THE LORD

The righteous shall never be removed:
but the wicked shall not inhabit the earth.

PROVERBS 10:30

The old apple tree had stood in the corner of the orchard for years. Its trunk was yards wide, and its branches stretched high into the sky. It had weathered many storms, even surviving being struck by lightning twice. It had long since retired from bearing fruit, but it cast shade over the yard and roof of the old farmhouse. Its roots dug deep into the soil, and nothing could move it from its place. The winds of time had long given up hopes of blowing it down, and the leaves thundered in defiance whenever a breeze kicked up.

As we dwell in Christ over the years, we lay roots which form a foundation which makes it impossible for us to be moved. Nothing can sway us if we plant ourselves completely in His love. If our roots are not in the Lord, we are shaken by the slightest thing, and we have no anchor to hold us in place. Christ invites us to take root there, we are there eternally, and nothing can affect us.

We are nurtured and strengthened by the grace of God, and we can depend on growing strong and secure in His care.

I place the seed of my faith in Your soil, O Lord. Nurture and feed it so that it might take root and grow. Help my faith to grow strong and tall in the light of Your love. Amen.

Strength in Weakness

A gracious woman retaineth honor:
and strong men retain riches.

PROVERBS 11:16

Judas Iscariot possessed qualities that Jesus considered worthy, or he never would have been selected as a disciple. Judas followed faithfully for the better part of three years as he shared in the ministry of Christ. At a time when he should have been most strong, he proved weak. He gave in to the temptation of the sparkle of silver, and he betrayed his friend and Lord. He had lived so very close to the true treasure—the love of Jesus Christ—and he threw it all away due to his weakness.

Everyone sins. That is sad, but true. Often we are weak when we want to be strong. It is vital that we hold on to the love of God in those times when we are most sorely tempted. God offers us His strength when our own strength is not enough.

All we need to do is pray for this strength, and it will be given to us. When we fall prey to sin and we allow it to control us, we join with Judas in betraying the truth of Christ. When we call on God to help us in our weakness, then we have found true wisdom and strength. If we will deal honestly with God, He will shower us with treasure which cannot be taken from us and honor which testifies to the glory of Christ.

O Lord, I pray that I might make You proud of me.
I will try to please You by my actions and praise You
with my words. Be with me, Father. Amen.

THE JOY OF GIVING

There is that scattereth, and yet increaseth;
and there is that withholdeth more than is meet,
but it tendeth to poverty.

PROVERBS 11:24

During the Great Depression, two families
shared a house in Pennsylvania. One family
occupied the upper floor, and the other family
lived on the lower. The family that lived downstairs
was always inviting people in to share what
they had. Whenever there was an opportunity for

them to help out, they would do so. No matter how much they gave, they always seemed to have enough. The family on the upper floor, however, scoffed at the way the downstairs family lived. They stored all extras in a locker in the pantry. They gave nothing away. It was not until they found that rats had gotten into their pantry that they were sorrowful for what they had done. Interestingly, the rats had not disturbed the downstairs pantry.

Selfishness leads to despair. True joy comes to us not from what we own but from what we are able to give to others. We were put on this earth to serve one another, and when we fail to do so, there is a price to pay. When we give what we have, God will bless us with more, and the blessing will be double because of the joy that giving brings.

Take what I have, Lord, and use it for Your glory.
I have nothing except what You have given me.
Help me to share from my abundance and to give
all that I can to those who are in need. Amen.

QUALITY

The wicked is snared by the transgression
of his lips: but the just shall come out of trouble. A man
shall be satisfied with good by the fruit of his mouth:
and the recompense of a man's hands shall be
rendered unto him. The way of a fool is right in his own
eyes: but he that hearkeneth unto counsel is wise.

PROVERBS 12:13–15

The man's hands moved over the wood with great love and care. The sharp tools never gouged or split, but they cut into the wood with precision. Each joint was perfect, and the result

was furniture of the highest quality. It made mass-produced furniture look pathetic in comparison. Many people were annoyed at the high price tag that much of the furniture carried, but people who recognized the quality of the skilled craftsmanship did not hesitate to pay the price. Each piece of furniture carried with it love and devotion to quality.

In our lives, when we produce that which is good, we will receive good compensation. When we produce inferior results, we cannot expect our reward to be great. We should strive to be perfectionists in our relationship with God. The same love and attention we pay Him will be what we can hope to receive. God is anxious to give His children good things, and we can be pleased with ourselves when we know He is giving us that which we are deserving of because we have tried to be the best we can be.

Almighty God, giver of good things, author of all life, help me to be a craftsman at the trade of life. Let me live a life of quality, giving attention to the finer points of life, and always giving glory and honor to You. Amen.

A KIND WORD

Heaviness in the heart of a man maketh it stoop:
but a good word maketh it glad.

PROVERBS 12:25

The day had been absolutely terrible. From the moment she had gotten up in the morning, things had gone wrong. Her son had dragged his feet just long enough to miss the bus. Then she had gotten caught in traffic and the car overheated. By the time she made it to work, she was over an hour late, and her boss had read her out. She had missed some important work the day before, which resulted in another lecture. She had dumped a cup of coffee on her skirt at lunch, then had broken a strap on one of her best pairs of shoes. Her car hadn't been ready when she went to pick it up, and she had to sit for an hour and a half until it was fixed. She thought, "If one more thing goes wrong, I will scream."

She ran up the steps to her house dreading the thought of making supper and cleaning up after the children, but as she opened the door, her heart leaped. The house was spotless, and dinner was waiting on the table. A note at her place read, "For the world's greatest mom. I love you." Suddenly, the weight of the day was lifted and things got much brighter.

It is the small things that often mean the most. We have great power at our disposal to make other people's lives so much brighter and happier. It is a joy to God when we use our power for good, and use it often.

A kind word can do so much, Lord. Help me to know when to say a kind word or offer a compliment. Let my words be a joy to those around me. Grace my speech with the light of Your love. Amen.

Waiting

Hope deferred maketh the heart sick:
but when the desire cometh, it is a tree of life.

PROVERBS 13:12

The snow fell furiously. Looking from the picture window, it was impossible even to see to the street. The wind blew the snow into great drifts, and travel had come to a standstill. Their son should have been home hours ago. He was driving in from the north, and they had hoped he would beat the storm. His mother sat transfixed by the blizzard, trying to gaze through it for some sign of her son. The father paced the room, mumbling occasionally about getting his coat and going out after him. The minutes ticked by into hours, and a tear trickled down the woman's cheek.

As darkness fell, two dim lights cut through the swirling white. A police truck pulled up in front of the house, and a young man jumped out. He ran through the front door and greeted his mother and father. His mother burst into tears, and his father grasped him in a bear-like embrace. The tense period of waiting was over, and the rejoicing began.

Waiting is never easy, but when we are anticipating something hoped for and it doesn't appear, we have to fight the disappointment, and sometimes fear. However, when our desire finally arrives, the joy is even greater. As we Christians await our eternal home, we grow more appreciative of it as time goes by. When it is finally ours, our joy will be overwhelming.

Patience is one thing I could use more of, Lord. As I look toward heaven, and long to be united with You, please fill me with Your patience, and allow me to learn all I can during my earthly stay. Amen.

Knowing the Truth

Whoso despiseth the word shall be destroyed:
but he that feareth the commandment shall be rewarded.

Proverbs 13:13

The woman sat at her desk reading the Bible over her lunch hour. One of her associates came up to her and said, "You don't really believe that garbage, do you? That's for weirdos and Jesus freaks." The woman looked up at the young man and said, "Have you ever read it? Do you know what it really says?"

"Hey, I don't have time to waste. You go on and read your fairy tales. I'll stick to reality."

"What happens if this is reality?" she asked, holding up the Bible.

"I'll worry about that when the time comes," he replied.

The time for a decision like that is now. If people reject the opportunity to read the scriptures and come to know the truth of Christ, then they will not get a second chance. Anyone who despises the word of God will have no place with God in the final times. It is the person who reads the Bible and lives their life accordingly, who will receive the reward of life everlasting. There is no greater book in existence, and it behooves each person to take its contents very seriously. Only a foolish person criticizes something that he or she has never read. It is the prudent person who makes time to investigate then draws a conclusion based on what they have experienced.

You have become real to me through the reading of Your Word. Assist me as I attempt to spread Your Word and bring others to the threshold of Your truth contained in the Old and New Testaments. Bless this effort. Amen.

Walking with Fools

The desire accomplished is sweet to the soul: but it is
abomination to fools to depart from evil.
He that walketh with wise men shall be wise: but a
companion of fools shall be destroyed.
Evil pursueth sinners:
but to the righteous good shall be repaid.

Proverbs 13:19–21

The young man was basically a good person, but he didn't have too many friends. He didn't seem to fit in with too many groups, so he found himself hanging around with the less desirable crowd. They accepted him just as he was. He knew there were times when he should have refused to go along with them, but it just didn't seem worth the risk. Now, he wasn't so sure. He was sitting in a police station, waiting to see what would happen. They had been picked up for vandalism, and even though he hadn't joined in the destruction, he was being held just the same.

If we choose to follow in the footsteps of fools, we will also have to suffer the consequences. When we walk along blindly, we are in danger of falling into sin. We must watch our steps and turn from that which is evil. It is our obligation to flee from sin and evil. If we keep company with fools, we will be destroyed by our own folly. It is much better for us to surround ourselves with those who are committed to what is right and good. Then we will not have to fear the result, for God will see our efforts, and He will reward us richly.

The company I keep influences me greatly, O God. Help me to discern who I should have as friends and who I should avoid. Let my company be a blessing to others, and lead me in all Your ways. Amen.

THE RIGHT ATTITUDE

A scorner seeketh wisdom, and findeth it not:
but knowledge is easy unto him that understandeth.

PROVERBS 14:6

A girl sat in the circle of the Bible study and listened to the lesson being taught. When asked what she thought, she replied, "This is stupid." She folded her arms across her chest and leaned back in her chair. She tuned out the rest of the lesson, and afterward she vowed never to return. A friend of hers said that she was being closed minded, but she said, "I don't have time for this junk. I want to know how to live better, just like everybody else, but I don't think this helps at all." The girl never gave the group a second chance.

It is interesting how some people can find the answers they are seeking in churches, while others seem unaffected. Partially, it has to do with the attitude we come with. If we are open to God and are willing to give Him a chance to disclose Himself, we will find Him. But if we come skeptically and we scorn His power to change lives, then we block His effectiveness. For every attempt He makes to reach us, we come up with some excuse to explain it away, and we come away as empty as when we arrived. If we come before God unwilling to listen to His Word, then we will never find wisdom, but when we are open-minded and willing to hear, God will grant us the knowledge we so desire.

I come before You with an open heart and an open mind. Grant that I might have knowledge which passes human understanding. Guard me from doubt and disbelief. Open my eyes to Your truth. Amen.

A HAPPY HEART

*Even in laughter the heart is sorrowful; and the
end of that mirth is heaviness.*

PROVERBS 14:13

She hated closing time at the bar. The crowds
had thinned and the lights were unplugged
and everything quieted down. It got too quiet.
She had to face the thought of going back to her
lonely apartment. She came to the bar to melt
into the noise and laughter. She could be charming
in the right setting. She could at least have a good

time for a few hours, but it always came to an abrupt end and she had to face her desperate unhappiness. She sometimes wished she could find a party which never ended, but that was senseless. Eventually she would have to come back to reality, and her problems would all be waiting for her when she did.

So many of our attempts to find happiness end in futility. We look in all the wrong places for fulfillment and happiness. We exert such energy pursuing good things, and we never attain them. The deep loneliness that we sometimes feel inside is a homesickness for our creator and heavenly home. When we take Christ into our hearts, we never have to face the loneliness which destroys. We stop looking for artificial answers, and we focus our attention on the one real answer: God. In Him, we find fulfillment and life.

O God, You have given my life such meaning. I no longer seek other answers, for I have found the one true answer. In Christ I have found everything I could ever desire. Thank You, O Lord. Amen.

SELF-CONTROL

A wise man feareth, and departeth from evil: but the
fool rageth, and is confident. He that is soon angry
dealeth foolishly: and a man of wicked devices is hated.

PROVERBS 14:16–17

The two players sat transfixed, their entire concentration on the chess board in front of them. The match had gone on for over an hour, and the heat was rising. Both players were looking for blood. They had played masterfully. Then, as quickly as it had started, it was over. A single wrong move resulted in defeat. The loser stood up

abruptly and wiped out the table. He stormed to the side of the room and slammed his hand into the wall, breaking bones and tearing the skin. He cried out in pain and rage and yelled for the room to be cleared. When the storm subsided, he sat alone in pain and shame, not only from his defeat but also from his childish display.

Self-control is an important part of the Christian's life. Christ had many occasions where He could have lost control and wreaked havoc on His enemies. That would have destroyed His mission on earth—to teach and love and provide an example for how we should live our lives. Anger is a natural reaction, but it cannot be allowed to take control of us. When we live by our passions, we live on the danger line, and eventually we will fall prey to sin. The wise person learns to respect the power of his or her emotions, and they depart from situations where they might lose control.

O Almighty God, save me from myself. When anger rises within my heart, help me to control it and channel it in constructive ways. Do not let me be a captive to my passions. Amen.

A Helping Hand

He that despiseth his neighbor sinneth:
but he that hath mercy on the poor, happy is he.

Proverbs 14:21

The yard had become a junk heap. There were rusty automobile parts, mattresses, pots and pans, bottles, and old magazines, not to mention the general rubbish that had accumulated.

The neighborhood was in an uproar. Maybe the police would shake them up. If something didn't happen soon, there were certain members of the neighborhood who were ready to take things into their own hands.

When the police came, they found an old couple who spoke very little English, and the husband suffered from many ailments. They wanted to keep their property nice, but they just weren't able to. When neighbors had complained they had tried to ask for help, but no one would pitch in. They felt totally helpless, and they were frightened by what might happen.

We can be so mean to each other without ever meaning to be. If more people would offer to help rather than threatening or bullying, our world would be a much more pleasant place. When we reach out to help others in need, we are displaying the love of Christ, which is at home within our hearts. When we refuse to show kindness to our neighbors, we are showing that Christ has no part in us.

Almighty God, may my actions always prove my love and devotion for You. Help me to share the love You have given to me with those who need it most. Make me a loving disciple, following Christ's example, and learning to love my neighbor as myself. Amen.

Strength in Trials

In the fear of the LORD is strong confidence:
and his children shall have a place of refuge.
The fear of the LORD is a fountain of life,
to depart from the snares of death.

PROVERBS 14:26–27

A young Russian was arrested for smuggling Bibles into area prisons. He stood before a tribunal for sentencing, and they shipped him off to a high security prison. Each day, he was taken to a warden who asked him if he was sorry for what he had done. His answer was always the same. Each time he said no, he was beaten then returned to his cell. Years went by, and the daily routine continued. The Russian prison hoped to break the spirit of the young man, but instead, an interesting thing happened. The prison held

thousands of prisoners, and over time, many of them were converted. Within the prison a great revival took place, all because the young man refused to renounce his faith in Christ.

The story is a familiar one. Christians have been persecuted over the centuries. When they withstood the torture and torment, they proved to be powerful witnesses to the truth of Christ.

A good knowledge of God gives us confidence so strong that nothing can shake it. The truth of God is a fountain of life, and by dwelling within it, we depart from sin and all its ramifications. When we stand fast in the truth of God, He will give us everything we need to hold on.

Be with me, God, to guide me, to support me,
to strengthen and love me. Never depart from me,
Lord, that I might stand fast in the face of every
trial and persecution. Allow me to be an example for
others. Amen.

Giving from the Heart

The sacrifice of the wicked is an abomination
to the Lord: but the prayer of the upright is his delight.

PROVERBS 15:8

There was a man who came out to church only on Easter. He felt that it "looked good" to put in an occasional appearance. He wanted people to think well of him and to know that he supported his church. Each year he made a big gift to the church, making sure that many key people were aware of the large amount. He bragged of his support and how much it meant to the church. Whenever he was asked to serve the church in any way, however, he couldn't find the time. Only when it was advantageous for him to be associated with the church would he consider it. His connection with the church was purely public relations.

Scripture says that God loves a cheerful giver, but He wants the giver to be sincere, also. Financial contributions are always important, but they are not nearly as important as the gift of self which each person should give. We are to give ourselves body, mind, and spirit to the work of

Christ's church. Anything less is not good enough. The gift given for the wrong reasons is an abomination to the Lord. The gift of the upright, rightly given, is a true joy to the Lord, and it is His delight.

O Lord, take my life and consecrate it to Your service. Take not only my gifts, but also my talents and resources as instruments for Your ministry. Guide me in the ways that I can best serve You, and grant me the wisdom to know where You want me to go. Amen.

Never Out of Sight

Hell and destruction are before the LORD:
how much more then the hearts of the children of men.

PROVERBS 15:11

A light plane crashed in the desert. The pilot survived the crash and began a long, hot trek toward civilization. He wandered for hours without seeing anything remotely man made.

As day turned to night, he began to think he had survived the crash just to die a slow, painful death. With morning light, he set out once more in search of rescue. When his last ounce of strength gave out, he sat down and began to cry. His sobs grew in intensity, and they merged with another sound. Controlling his emotions, he looked up to see a jeep approaching in the distance. He bowed his head to say a quick thank you, then waved to the driver of the vehicle.

There are times when we feel that we must surely be out of God's sight, or at least out of His favor. It is comforting to know that God sees everything that goes on no matter where it is. God can see into the very depths of hell, so it is no great wonder that He can see into our hearts to know what we are feeling and thinking. Our lives are open to our creator, and at the time when we think we have no hope, the grace of the Lord will reach down to us and let us know that we are saved. God will never leave us, no matter how far we may go.

Be with me, Father, as I walk along the many paths which make up my life. When I lose my way and turn from the one true path, wait patiently for me to return, and keep me ever in Your watchful eye. Amen.

Blessed Are the Peacemakers

A wrathful man stirreth up strife:
but he that is slow to anger appeaseth strife.

PROVERBS 15:18

The first pitch had been an accident. It had slipped from the pitcher's grip and had sailed at the head of the batter. Angry stares were exchanged, but nothing more. The very next inning, the opposing pitcher threw at the batter. The batter tossed aside his bat, and he charged the pitcher. Both benches emptied and a brawl broke out. Players and coaches were ejected from the game, and tempers were allowed to cool before the umpires allowed play to resume.

It's a common occurrence and a sad one. Grown men trying to start fights is silly, and it destroys the integrity of the sport. But once a person's pride is damaged, they will stop at nothing to get revenge. Spiteful people live to stir up strife. It is the prudent person, one who holds his or her anger and stifles his or her pride, who brings forth peace. If we could learn to care less about ourselves and more about others, there would be fewer occasions when we would cause discord. It is the person who loves God who also loves peace. The peacemakers are the true disciples of Christ. To the person who refuses to stir up strife, there will come a great reward.

You have blessed the peacemakers, Almighty God. Please number me among them. Wherever I can be used, let me be an agent of Your love and peace. Send me where You would have me to go, O Lord. Amen.

GOD'S FORGIVENESS

By mercy and truth iniquity is purged:
and by the fear of the LORD men depart from evil.

PROVERBS 16:6

She felt so much better. She hadn't meant to hurt anyone, and she'd carried the guilt around with her long enough. The minute she heard about the fire, she remembered having left the coffeepot plugged in. Two people were injured, and she had been frightened to speak up. Then her supervisor had been blamed, and she felt so guilty. She tried

to ignore it, but it kept nagging at her. She finally had to say something, not only to clear her supervisor, but also to clear her conscience.

Confession is good for the soul. We cannot hope to improve our lives when we walk around burdened by guilt and shame. When we admit our wrongdoing, we are able to begin anew with a clean slate. We can be so thankful that God forgives us the things we do wrong. Without that forgiveness, there would be no way for us to be united with Him. When we receive God's blessed forgiveness, it is as though we never sinned at all. God forgives and forgets, and once God has wiped our sin away, it is gone for good. Only when we are wise enough to admit our sin can we hope to be cleansed of it. God will not force us to come to Him. Only when we seek Him out and confess our sins to Him will he forgive us and make us new.

Heavenly Father, forgive me for the many things that I have done wrong. Help me to begin anew, starting fresh, and committed to doing what is right and good. Lead me in the paths of righteousness, Lord. Amen.

LITTLE KINDNESSES

The wise in heart shall be called prudent:
and the sweetness of the lips increaseth learning.

PROVERBS 16:21

There was a small boy who always looked out for the feelings of others. Whenever the children would begin to tease or taunt another child, the small boy would defend the victim and offer comforting words. If a child fell or was hurt, the small boy ran to help. Whenever one of the children was in need of cheering up, the boy was right there with a kind word. All the adults said

that he had the soul of an older man, and they claimed he was wise beyond his years.

Kindness is such a small thing, and yet too few people practice it. When a person is kind it causes others to sit up and take notice. The person who is kind and loving provides an example of what Christ wants for all of us. We enjoy being with kind people. They make us feel good and they cheer us up. They are special people indeed, and it is well for us to join their ranks. God loves to see His children offer kindness to each other. Kindness is contagious, and we should always strive to cause an epidemic of loving and giving. Christians should be the first to be kind, to show the power of God in their lives to make a difference. Wisdom of the heart is the love of God, and it is the greatest gift we can hope to share with others.

I want to sow the seeds of Your love wherever I go, dear Father. Make me an agent of kindness and consideration. Help me to lift the spirits of other people and to make sure that they know joy all their lives. Amen.

FORGIVE AND FORGET

He that covereth a transgression seeketh love;
but he that repeateth a matter separateth very friends.

PROVERBS 17:9

"You never let me forget, do you? Look,
I said I was sorry a hundred times. I lied,
I was wrong. It won't ever happen again!"

It happened every time they got into an
argument. He knew he had done wrong, but he
had asked forgiveness a dozen times. It would cool
down, but then somehow it would come up and
start another argument. If only he would let go of
it, but no, he always held it over his head. It hurt
to know that he wasn't forgiven. He had blown it
and was truly sorry, but to be reminded of it over
and over made him feel like a heel. He didn't
know how much longer he could hear about it
before it would begin to affect their friendship.

True forgiveness only occurs when we treat
the subject as a closed matter. If we bring up old

hurts whenever feelings fly, then we have never really forgiven. To hold a grudge is to build a wall between yourself and another person. Forgiveness breaks down walls. Christ came to break down walls and lead people to reconciliation. Before true healing can occur, though, we must let loose of all old hurts and start fresh. Forgiveness gives us the clean start we need to heal all wounds. With God's help, we can grow closer than ever before.

Teach me how to drop old hurts into the sea of forgetfulness and truly forgive those who have harmed me. Fill me with Your grace, that I might learn how to be graceful to others. Amen.

PERSISTENT LOVE

Whoso rewardeth evil for good,
evil shall not depart from his house.

PROVERBS 17:13

She had tried everything she knew. She had
been kind, she had gone out of her way to be
friendly, she had offered her rides home, she had
bent over backwards to help her out, and she still
was rotten to her. She couldn't understand why
anybody would want to be so mean. Her best
friend had told her that the girl was spreading
terrible rumors about her. This very night she had
tried to be friendly, and the girl had called her
names. Some of her friends said that the girl was
just jealous of her, but still, that didn't give her the
right to be so nasty.

It is hard to understand why people have to be so unkind. We can try everything we know to be nice, and still there are some who will not respond in kind. Those people are to be pitied, for they will never know happiness or peace. There is something that causes them to be terribly unhappy, and they vent their sadness on those around them. Christ enables us to return good for good, and even good for evil, but He never likes to see us return evil for good. Happy and content is the person who spreads happiness, but sad will be the person who spreads evil, for the wrong done will never be escaped.

O Lord, make me a doer of good works, and help me to avoid doing things which are wrong or hurtful. Help me to understand the people who do me evil, and guide me to try to help them whenever I can. Amen.

GOOD MEDICINE

A merry heart doeth good like a medicine:
but a broken spirit drieth the bones.

PROVERBS 17:22

Two men went into the hospital at about the
same time, having suffered similar heart
attacks. One of the men grew depressed and
irritable. He felt betrayed by his own body and saw
his affliction as a sign of weakness. His attitude was
sour and he cursed his fate. The other man took it
in stride. He kidded with everyone who came to
visit him, and he laughed long and hard. He refused
to be brought down by his plight. Instead,
he occupied his time cheering up other patients
and chatting with the staff. The first man grew
weak and frail. The other man left the hospital in
good health, and resumed his old life quickly.

The way we face life has a lot to do with how
good we will feel about it. If we are negative,
then life will be a burden, but if we are positive,
life will seem like the greatest gift we've ever
known. Happiness is contagious. When we are
happy it spreads. However, sadness is contagious,

too, and when we are gloomy, we spread a gray cloud over all the people we meet. A positive spirit is like a powerful medicine. It has a great deal of power to heal. It is so much better to face life with joy than to let life get you down. The person who feels that life is bad will wither and fail. God gave us life to enjoy, and He blesses us when we embrace it with happiness and contentment.

Fill my heart with joy that never ends. Let it overflow from my life to touch the lives of those around me. Make me a source of happiness for everyone I meet. Grace my countenance with a smile, bathed in the light of Your love. Amen.

LETTING GO

Through desire a man, having separated himself,
seeketh and intermeddleth with all wisdom.
A fool hath no delight in understanding, but that
his heart may discover itself.

PROVERBS 18:1—2

I have always had the problem of turning a situation over to God and then pulling it back and trying to handle it myself. As much as I trust God, I find myself holding back and trying to do things by myself. I know in my heart that God is in complete control and that there is no place better for my problem than in His care. That never stops me from meddling. I foolishly think that I can do every bit as well on my own. Then, when things fall apart, I chastise myself for my stupidity.

Wisdom comes to the man or woman who can trust God totally and give up their problems to Him. Peace of mind and heart is a rare and valuable quality, and the person who truly trusts God will find it. There is absolutely nothing we can do better than God, except mess up a situation. If we will learn to let go of our trials and let God work them out, then we will come to know the real meaning of faith. Faith is the confidence of things not seen, the assurance of things hoped for. When we trust God, He will do everything we ask, and our faith will be made rock solid. Foolish people think they know best, but the person who admits limitations is well on the road to wisdom.

I am so confident of my ability to control my life, and yet there are times when I have just had enough. Let me learn to turn to You for strength and wisdom. You know the way, and You wait to lead me through every trial. Amen.

ARROGANCE

Before destruction the heart of man is haughty,
and before honor is humility.

PROVERBS 18:12

The opposing team came strutting out onto the court in brand new matching uniforms. The girls warmed up, and they acted cocky. They had been champions two years running, and you could tell that they thought they would have no trouble with the rag-tag band which was there to face them. The other girls looked a little lost on the volleyball court, and they wore whatever shorts and T-shirts they could throw together. The other team was intimidating, just by their appearance, never mind their attitude.

The games were close, but when the smoke cleared, David had once again knocked off Goliath. The former champs were not quite so haughty now. They looked down at their feet and offered insincere and unconvincing congratulations. Their spirit broken, they headed out of the gymnasium, while the giant killers reveled in their victory.

Sinners kid themselves into believing that they are above the silly faith of Christians. They think that they are too good, too smart for God. When they find out they are wrong, they act as if they had never been told. Humility is a wonderful virtue. It assures the person that they can never be knocked down, because they were never too high in the first place. God blesses the person who realizes they are no better than anyone else.

You have created so many different kinds of people, dear Lord. Help me to love them all equally, never thinking that I am better than any of them. Grant that I might see Your image in every human being. Amen.

THE POWER OF THE TONGUE

Death and life are in the power of the tongue: and they that love it shall eat the fruit thereof.

Pilate looked out over the crowds of people. So, it had come to this. People who usually had no use for him were now coming to him, looking for him to pass judgment on one of their own.

It was exhilarating to have such power. With a word, he could bestow life or death. The Nazarene seemed totally unimpressed by his power, but the crowd knew better. They knew that his word was law! No matter how many times he was called upon to pronounce sentence, he still grew tense with excitement. This was power, and he loved it.

There is power in our words. Our tongues are like two-edged swords. They can protect and defend, or they can cut down and destroy. We are in control of them. Sadly, many people act as if it was the other way around; their tongues controlled their minds. As Christians, it is vital that we learn to control our tongues. James compares the tongue to a rudder. When a rudder is left untended, the ship flounders. Likewise, when our tongues move uncontrolled, the result is disaster. A wise person keeps a firm control over his or her words. Only words of life and light should be spoken, and with God's help we can hope to always have such graceful speech.

O Lord, take control of the rudder and steer this humble vessel. Use the words of my mouth to minister to the needs of others. Let the will of my heart always precede the words of my mouth. Amen.

A SECOND CHANCE

The discretion of a man deferreth his anger;
and it is his glory to pass over a transgression.

PROVERBS 19:11

This was the third home she had been placed in, but it was by far the best. The first place she went, they tried to lock her in her room after dark. They punished her severely and even hit her. She had run away so many times that they put her back in the orphanage. The second home was like a hurricane. Everybody was fighting all the time.

She had called the director of the home for girls in tears, and they had come to get her. This new place was different, though. The people acted like they cared. The fact that she had run away so much and that she had been sent to reformatory two times didn't seem to make a difference to her new folks. They acted like they trusted her, and when she had asked them why, they had told her that all the other stuff was in the past. They would trust her until she gave them reason not to. She decided right then and there that she was going to try never to give them any reason.

It is so important for us to forgive people their past sins. When we mistrust someone because of their past, we apply a stigma to them that they fight all of their lives. It is better to learn to forgive, and to keep forgiving, so that the person can know that there is no judgment which will come from us. Judgment will come from the Lord. What should come from us is open and honest love and the gift of a second chance.

Lord, let me forgive those whom I meet, and grant that I might learn to forgive others as You have forgiven me. Amen.

IN GOD'S WILL

There are many devices in a man's heart;
nevertheless the counsel of the LORD, that shall stand.

PROVERBS 19:21

A woman asked a question of her pastor. "What if Moses had refused to face Pharaoh? Or if Abraham had refused to obey God's command to slay Isaac? Or if Christ had decided to follow His will in the Garden of Gethsemane rather than God's?" The pastor reflected on the question for a moment and then said, "I suppose God would have

found someone else. If God wants something done, it will be done. His way will be established, not the way of man."

It is important to realize that God will work in spite of us when He cannot work through us. We need to heed His call carefully, for if we are indecisive or resistant, He might just go elsewhere, looking for someone who will follow Him. God's will is supreme, and it is a privilege to be a part of it. We may think of millions of directions for our lives to go, but if we put our trust in God, He will be faithful to set us upon the best path, and He will walk beside us every step of the way. It is a great comfort to know that God is in control, and that in the end, everything will be just as He intended it to be.

God, I do not presume to pretend that I understand everything that You do. Your will is far beyond my comprehension. Thank You for loving me enough to make me a part of Your great creation. Walk with me, and be with me this day and all the days to come. Amen.

Look Up

*It is an honor for a man to cease from strife:
but every fool will be meddling.*

PROVERBS 20:3

She wished she could be like her husband. Nothing ever seemed to get to him. He took everything in stride, and he acted as though he hadn't a care in the world. She, on the other hand, worried about everything. She was positive that if there was something that could possibly go wrong, it would. She didn't mean to be negative, but she couldn't help it. She wanted to be able to let go of her doubts and fears, but so far she hadn't been able to.

It's sometimes hard to realize that God gave us life as a gift. Many times it feels like such a burden. God never wants us to suffer unnecessarily. Part of the message that Christ brought to this world was that no one had to face problems alone. God is with us always. Another part of His message was that nothing on this earth is important other than our relationship to God and to our neighbor. Job, finances, illness, and a hundred other things create stress in our lives, but when compared with the bigger picture of eternal life, they are totally insignificant. As Christians, we need to learn to look at the world through eternity-eyes, rather than temporal-eyes. Our home is in heaven, and everything that happens to us now means nothing, so long as we have our relationships in order.

Lord, I get sidetracked so easily. I let the silliest things bring me down. Help me to see everything in its proper perspective. Grant me peace of mind which never ends. Amen.

STAYING THE COURSE

The sluggard will not plow by reason of the cold;
therefore shall he beg in harvest, and have nothing.

PROVERBS 20:4

There is a famous children's story about a little red hen who searched for other barnyard residents to help her bake bread. No matter where she went, all the other animals had some reason why they couldn't pitch in and help. Finally, she decided to bake the bread by herself, and soon the entire barnyard was filled with the enticing aroma of her coop-baked bread. When the other animals smelled the fine bread, they flocked around the chicken coop with their mouths watering. The hen peeked her head out and announced, "Everyone who

helped make the bread gets a big slice with butter!" Whereupon, she proceeded to eat hers in front of a group of regretful loafers.

How sorry a day it will be when we are called to stand before the judgment throne of God if we have not chosen to follow His commandments. He has asked us to do what we know we should, and often we disobey, not through an evil spirit, but because of laziness. Just as the animals in the story, though, we can hope to receive no more than we were willing to give in this life. If we give nothing, then nothing will we receive. If we give much, our Father in heaven will heap an unending supply of good things upon us.

When a call comes for obedience or service, let me be the first to raise my hand to volunteer, O Lord. I do not want to be left outside in the last days. Welcome me into Your holy presence, Father. Amen.

THE MIRACLE OF CREATION

The hearing ear, and the seeing eye,
the LORD hath made even both of them.

PROVERBS 20:12

He stood looking on in awe. His son, his firstborn, was coming into the world, and he was a part of it. He stood by his wife's head, and together they shared the wonder of the experience. He had often doubted whether God existed, but now all of his doubts were gone. He looked on at the perfect little creation. Each finger and toe was a testament to God's loving existence. The miracle of life was overwhelming. It was inconceivable that something like this could happen by chance. Only a master artist of incomprehensible power and glory could come up with something so fine as human life.

When we look at God's creation, it is difficult to question anything about Him. There is so much to wonder at in the world. As we learn more and more, it should not make us skeptical of God. Quite the contrary, it should convince us that there is a grand author to all creation, and that His power is far beyond our wildest imagination. Only a foolish person would deny God's existence in the face of such remarkable evidence. To see God, all we must do is open our eyes and look around. His signature is on each one of his creations. He is right there for the person who has eyes to see and ears to hear. God is all around us.

O Lord, You are indeed everywhere. I look to the sky, and Your beauty and wonder meet my eye. I look around, and I see You in the faces of those I meet. I look inward, and thankfully, I see You in my heart. Amen.

GOSSIP

He that goeth about as a talebearer revealeth secrets:
therefore meddle not with him that flattereth with his lips.

PROVERBS 20:19

A man was seen coming and going from a
married woman's house. Her neighbor
watched with fascination and concocted elaborate
tales which she shared with her friends as truth.
There was no evidence any more incriminating
than the fact that the young man came regularly,
but the rumor was that the woman was having an
affair. The "news" spread like wildfire, and wind of
it eventually got back to the woman's husband.
He confronted her in anger and hurt. The woman
defended herself well. The young man she was
seeing was her own brother, who came to the
house to study in between his classes. The senseless
words of gossip caused unnecessary pain to other
people, and planted a seed of doubt which caused
great trouble.

There is no such thing as a harmless gossip.
Gossip is wrong. It is talking about someone in a
negative way who has no chance to defend himself.

It is usually based on half-truths and sparse information. It isn't done to build someone up. It is only done to tear someone down. When we tell false stories about another person, we are stealing from them in the worst way. We take away dignity and honor, and we throw dirt on their reputation. It is an evil that God despises because of its basic cruelty. Lovers of the Lord are lovers of all His children. Therefore, we should speak of our sisters and brothers only as we would speak of the Lord Himself.

May my words be ever praiseworthy. Let no foulness or gossip pass from my lips, O Lord. Amen.

FRIVOLITY

He that loveth pleasure shall be a poor man: he that
loveth wine and oil shall not be rich.

PROVERBS 21:17

It was his first real job. He was making a good
salary, and he could now afford to live in style.
He decorated his apartment, threw fantastic
parties, and stayed out all night on the weekends
seeking new and different thrills. He moved into
the fast lane and spent money as fast as he could
earn it. He had never done so much before in his
life. He bought all the things he'd ever wanted and
many things he'd never dreamed of. He traveled
and bought expensive gifts for his friends.
Everything was as good as it could possibly be.
Until he was fired.

He had never believed his party could come to
an end, but his lifestyle intruded on his work, and
it led to his firing. Now he had nothing. No savings,
no support, and no way to pay bills. His dream
come true turned into a nightmare. He felt sick.

When we live for fun and self-indulgence,
we live for nothing lasting at all. Our lives need

meaning. They need a foundation. They need God. If we devote ourselves to Him, then we don't have time for frivolous endeavors, which cause us to be selfish and wasteful. God will help us to live wisely and prudently. He will help us to know what is right and what is wrong. He will be faithful to do all of this, if we will only consent to put our trust in Him.

I do want to put my faith in You, God. I know that on my own I will give in to temptations which are selfish and foolish. Protect me from myself, O Lord. Guide me in the paths of what is right and good. Amen.

OPPORTUNITY

He coveteth greedily all the day long:
but the righteous giveth and spareth not.

PROVERBS 21:26

His vow had been that when he made it big, he was going to help people like the ones he had grown up around. They had been poor mining people in closed mining towns, and they had small hope for anything but a dismal future. He remembered his vow while he was climbing, but every time he thought of using any of his wealth to help them, he balked. The only way to make money was to invest money, he told himself. The more he made, the more he would be able to give. He never gave. He could never let go of any of his wealth for even a short time. No amount was enough. He could have given a million dollars to the town and never missed it, but the bug had bitten, and greed was the ruling force in his life. He died financially rich but spiritually and morally poor. All his good intentions went to the grave with him, and the people who so desperately could have used his help found none.

God has blessed us with riches for one reason. It is not because we are deserving or because He is rewarding us, it is simply that we might give it to others who need it more than we do. Giving is the heart of a Christian. We should take every opportunity that comes our way to give of our time, talents, and resources. God blesses the giver, both in this life, and the eternal life to come.

Take from me the spirit to covet and hold. Open my heart and my mind to the needs that I can do something to fill. I give to You everything that I have and everything that I am. Use me as You see fit. Amen.

PRIDEFUL WAYS

There is no wisdom nor understanding
nor counsel against the LORD.

PROVERBS 21:30

Lucifer, the most perfect of all of God's creation, looked to place himself on the same level as God. He wanted to be worshipped for his perfection, and he conspired against God. He grew jealous of the Lord, and he began to work against Him. He led one-third of the angels in revolt against the Lord, and he and his followers were cast from heaven.

The sin of pride is a dangerous one. It makes us think we are better than we really are. It leads us to judge others, and it makes us resentful of what we are not given. We disregard God's commands, and we begin to think only of ourselves. We close off all that is right and good, and we make ourselves out to be our own god. We worship ourselves in subtle ways, and we rebel against the Lord by denying His will. Just like Lucifer, when we come before God, He will cast us away from Him. There is no place for sin in heaven, and the sin of pride is one of the worst. Sin finds its seed in selfishness, the sister of pride. God knows what is going on inside our hearts and minds. He can see right through us. If we will put our trust in Him and keep Him always as our Lord, then He will guide us away from pride and into a respect for all His children.

All secrets are open to You, O Lord. You know our comings and goings, and no thought goes by You unnoticed. Forgive my thoughts of pride and arrogance and lead me to a life of humble obedience and worship. Amen.

A LEGACY OF WISDOM

Remove not the ancient landmark,

which thy fathers have set.

PROVERBS 22:28

When the neighbors decided to sell their land, they thought little of it. Now, it was a major dispute. The neighbors were claiming that they had ownership of part of their land. It would have been a moot point twenty years before. His father had set large stone pillars on the property line, and a fence stretched from one to the other. They had marked the boundaries clearly

and concisely, but they had been removed long ago, and now there was nothing to show where the line was. The property deeds had somehow been lost, and it looked like the court might find in favor of the neighbors.

Sometimes we devalue the things our parents have done. We assume they acted impetuously and without cause. We lose touch with their wisdom and their desires. We destroy their legacy to us, bit by bit. This is most true of the teachings they gave us when we were young. Parents do their best to bring up their children in the best way possible. They do what they can and hope that some of it sticks. Our heavenly Father does the same thing. God has given us a legacy, which has stretched over thousands of years. The tales of the Bible should give us instruction on how we should live our lives and what we should avoid. Often we choose to ignore the instruction, thinking that it is outdated. God's truth never grows out of date, and His instruction is as a lamp unto our feet.

Lord God, forgive me when I think that I know more than those who have gone before me. Help me to see the wisdom of history, especially my personal history, that I might discern all the treasures that have been left for me. Amen.

A Great Deal

Buy the truth, and sell it not;
also wisdom, and instruction, and understanding.

PROVERBS 23:23

It looked like a great deal. He had wanted a new camera for a long time, and when he saw the one he wanted for $300 less than any other price he had found, he jumped at the chance. It worked well for a couple of weeks, but then the shutter stuck. After that, the pictures came out foggy. The lens didn't seat properly on the face of the camera, and the film started jamming. It didn't take long to realize that he had been taken. The camera he bought was nothing but junk. He had paid a foolishly low price, and he had been made a fool of.

There are so many things in our lives that look good, but they are really inferior. Fame, wealth, prestige, looks, all seem like they are wonderful things to have, but they fade away and leave us with nothing. Truth, wisdom, and understanding are costly, but they are worth anything we have to give. They fill us with an inner treasure, which does not fade. There is nothing greater for us to devote ourselves to. God will guide us to wisdom and understanding if we will ask Him to. He blesses anyone who sincerely tries to find truth. With God on our side, we can rest assured that we will attain our goal. Once attained, we will never let go of the riches we have been blessed with.

There is a lot in this world that has no value. Keep me from giving myself to those things. Make me desire truth, wisdom, instruction, and understanding. I love You, Father, and I want to do what is right. Bless my efforts. Amen.

WHEN IT COUNTS

*If thou faint in the day
of adversity, thy strength is small.*
PROVERBS 24:10

They had rehearsed the play a hundred times. A month of hard work was quickly coming to its payoff. The play opened to a packed house, and the actors and actresses waited anxiously for the curtain to rise. The lines had been memorized, the costumes fitted, the makeup put on and taken off repeatedly, the lights were in place, and the performers were in their places. The production went smoothly most of the way, but one actor completely forgot his lines. Instead of covering for himself, he froze. The other actors covered as well as they could, and the play finished without

further incident. The actor was replaced after a few more bungled performances, and the play went on to receive rave reviews.

The Christian life is a preparation for the glory which is to come. We rehearse our parts every time we follow in the footsteps of Christ. It is important that we know our parts well before we go to the judgment seat of Christ. Those who know their parts well have nothing to fear. But if we freeze and are found lacking, then we will be unfit for the Kingdom. Good actors and actresses dedicate themselves totally to their craft. Christians must do the same. Our faith must completely guide our lives. If that is true, then we, too, will meet with rave reviews in the last days.

I want to be skilled in the ways of righteousness and light, Almighty God. Help me to know how You would have me to walk. Help me to be faithful to practice my faith continually. Amen.

GREAT REWARDS

*Fret not thyself because of evil men, neither be thou
envious at the wicked; for there shall be no reward to the
evil man; the candle of the wicked shall be put out.*

PROVERBS 24:19–20

It made him so mad sometimes. He worked
diligently at his job, doing everything in his
power to make sure that each thing was done right.
However, the man he worked with couldn't have
cared less. If things were substandard, it didn't
bother him at all. What made it really bad was that
the rest of the company respected the work that the
pair produced. No one knew that it was all because
of him that things were done well. His partner was
more than willing to share the glory, but he
wouldn't carry his end of the load. It was infuriating
to do all the work and then share the credit.

His efforts were not in vain, nor did they go
unnoticed. When promotions came around, he
was moved up into a managerial position, while
his former partner stayed right where he was.

Often, it seems like the wrong people get all
the glory. We try to do our very best, and we

receive no credit at all. It is good to know that our Father in heaven knows everything that is going on, and one day we will be promoted to our heavenly reward. God blesses those of His children who do what they know they should. Those who slack off can hope for nothing more than His wrath, for He will not abide by the person who gives less than their very best.

I want to do the best in every situation. Help me to find my full potential and to use it in Your service. Lead me where I need most to go, and show me how I can be of the most usefulness. Amen.

SOLVING THE MYSTERY

It is the glory of God to conceal a thing:
but the honor of kings is to search out a matter.
The heaven for height, and the earth for depth,
and the heart of kings is unsearchable.

PROVERBS 25:2-3

He loved mysteries. He would lock himself in his room and read detective stories for hours. He would take notes so that he could outsmart the detective and solve the mystery first. Any kind of puzzle fascinated him, and he threw himself into whatever mystery lay before him.

Most people are fascinated by a good mystery. We like to be challenged and to give our minds exercise. There is no greater mystery in this life than the mystery of God. He is a puzzle beyond our comprehension, but His greatest desire is that we will try to know Him as best we can. He longs for us to devote our lives to an understanding of His will and ways. He has given us the holy scriptures to read and contemplate, and they hold both questions and answers which can occupy a lifetime. If we will work to unlock the mysteries of God, He will help us and lead us to ever-greater understanding. We must spend time daily with the Lord in order to know Him more. We need not expect answers immediately, but we can live with the questions and struggle out their solutions. No greater challenge awaits us, but its reward is finer than the purest gold if we will face it.

For every answer I receive, there is another question to take its place. Grant me the determination to pursue You with all my heart and mind. Give me the key to unlock the mystery of Your love and grace, O Lord. Amen.

REFRESHMENT

As the cold of snow in the time of harvest,
so is the faithful messenger to them that send him:
for he refresheth the soul of his masters.

PROVERBS 25:13

There was no doubt about it, harvest time was the hardest time of year. The planting and tilling and weeding were difficult, but harvest required every ounce of strength and stamina a soul could muster. When the days were cool, it made the job so much more pleasant, but when it was hot, there was no worse job on earth. The fields baked in the hot sun, and you baked also. Many a farmer came to his end out in the fields at harvest time when the sun was hot. This year was great. The snow was moving south from the hills, and the air off the plains was cold and brisk. Working in weather like this made you feel alive. It was refreshing and made you feel like you could work forever without stopping.

The breath of the Lord is like that. When we live without it, we are amazed at how hard this life is. We feel completely drained and exhausted by the simplest of tasks. When we have the Lord in our lives, however, He gives us strength and renews our stamina. With God all things are possible, and when His Spirit is in our hearts, we feel as if we can last forever without pausing. We are made conquerors with Christ, and nothing can defeat us.

Renew me, Father, in those times when I feel that I cannot go on. Forgive me when I try to live life all by myself, turning from Your loving care. Give me Your Spirit that I might rise above the struggles of this life and claim the victory won for me by Christ. Amen.

LOVING OUR ENEMIES

If thine enemy be hungry, give him bread to eat;
and if he be thirsty, give him water to drink:
for thou shalt heap coals of fire upon his head,
and the LORD shall reward thee.

PROVERBS 25:21–22

The air was strangely silent. The last of the mortar shell had exploded, and the gunfire had ceased. The skirmish had gone on for hours. A patrol moved forward to check for the enemy, and as they rounded a bend, an enemy soldier lay

bleeding in the path. One of the soldiers raised his rifle to shoot the man, but his partner told him to stop. The man was in bad shape, and he needed help. All the killing was senseless, and it seemed criminal to shoot someone who had one foot in the grave. The soldiers carried the hurt enemy toward his own side, and they bandaged his wound. They left him with water and food, and they went on their way. In the center of a terrible war, the two men felt like they had found something right to do and they had done it.

If someone would do us harm, that is something that they will have to answer for. God has said we should love everyone, and we are called to serve not only our friends but our enemies as well. We will answer to God for our actions, and our enemies will answer for theirs as well. It is vital that we have nothing to be ashamed of in that final time. We must not act like those who would hurt us. When we treat them with love, we make their sin doubly dark, and the Lord rejoices in our loving kindness.

I have difficulty loving those who love me, Father, so I definitely need Your help to love my enemies. Show me what is good in them that I might respond with concern and affection. Amen.

DEFENDING THE FAITH

The legs of the lame are not equal:
so is a parable in the mouth of fools.

PROVERBS 26:7

The discussion always came around to
religion. She was a devout woman who read
her Bible daily, prayed morning and evening, and
went to church weekly. He, on the other hand,
was neither a believer nor a nonbeliever; he just
liked to argue. The problem was that he had read
the Bible and he knew it inside out. She would try
to explain her beliefs to him, and he would tear

them apart using scripture as his support. It always made her angry to the point of tears. She knew he was twisting scripture to make it say what he wanted it to say, but she didn't have the knowledge she needed to combat it. He took the Bible and made it into a joke.

When foolish people get ahold of the Bible, they can do some pretty terrible things with it. They twist its meaning and they use it for selfish reasons. Nonbelievers love to take the Bible and quote it out of context. They like to misinterpret it in order to make believers appear foolish. How much more so they will look before the judgment seat of God when they are called upon to explain themselves. God gave us the Bible as a comfort and a support, not as a topic for debate. If we will spend time in scripture, it will prove a faithful friend, and no one will be able to take its riches from us.

I fall into the trap of defending my faith, Father, when I have nothing to defend. Christ defended Himself with His resurrection, and He needs no further defense. Help me to remember not to argue my faith, but to live it. Amen.

JUST JOKING

As a mad man who casteth firebrands, arrows,
and death, so is the man that deceiveth his neighbor,
and saith, Am not I in sport?

PROVERBS 26:18—19

A man had the habit of making fun of people as a joke. He would often lapse into extremely poor taste, and he offended regularly. When people would react in anger, he would accuse them of not having a sense of humor, and he would say, "Hey, I'm only kidding. You know how much I think of you." Then he would turn around and insult them all over again. He thought that he was being immensely humorous, and many people laughed at his jokes, just so long as they weren't the target of them.

There is no such thing as a harmless joke at the expense of another human being's feelings or dignity. Christ calls us to respect and love one another, and we have no right to do anything that might prove hurtful. Our words should build each other up, not provide a stumbling block. A lot of cruelty has been masked as jokes throughout the centuries, but one day God will judge what was funny, and what was evil. It is the duty of every person of God to weigh the impact of their words and to speak in ways which are a blessing rather than a curse. The Lord rejoices when our words are sweet and gentle, but His wrath is kindled by words which burn and cause anguish.

Lord, fill my mouth with the sweet sounds that are pleasing to You. In a world of such unkindness, let my speech reflect a love and caring that is foreign to most and a haven of peace to all. Amen.

INNER BEAUTY

Burning lips and a wicked heart
are like a potsherd covered with silver dross.

PROVERBS 26:23

Every head turned toward the door when she walked in. She was breathtaking. Her hair was long and beautiful. Her face had fine, gentle features, and she was tall and slender. She moved with a quiet grace, and she knew all the right moves. Many people gravitated toward her, and she basked in the attention. One young man walked up to her and tried to engage her in a conversation. She took one look at him and began laughing.

"Go away, you worm. I don't want to even be seen talking to you!"

Throughout the evening, she repeatedly dealt with people with equal measures of contempt.

Her gorgeous exterior merely covered an evil and corrupt interior, blinded with self-love and conceit.

We can take garbage and dress it up on a silver platter, but when we are finished, it is still garbage. What is on the outside matters very little. It is what is on the inside which is more important. God created each of us with a spirit, which is in His image. Looks, dress, and actions have little to do with who we are. It is what is in our hearts, which matters most. Wickedness can be masked, but God will see right through the façade. The pure in heart and right-minded are a joy to God, and it doesn't matter one bit what those people look like on the outside.

Lord, cleanse me inside. Make me a new creation in Your love and grace. Help me to put aside vanity over looks and appearances. Let my only concern be what is in my heart. Amen.

HONESTY

Whoso diggeth a pit shall fall therein:
and he that rolleth a stone, it will return upon him.
A lying tongue hateth those that are afflicted by it;
and a flattering mouth worketh ruin.

PROVERBS 26:27–28

S he couldn't believe what was happening.
She had accepted a date for Friday night from
a man she was seeing off and on. Then, out of the
blue, her boss had asked her out. She had dreamed
of that happening ever since she got the job.

She reluctantly called her date for the evening
and told him that she had become very ill and that
she wouldn't be able to go out. Then she prepared
herself for her evening with her boss. It was a
wonderful evening, and she kept trying to tell
herself that what she had done was perfectly fine.

They were riding the elevator up to her floor,
and she was anticipating a nice ending to the
evening in her apartment. When the elevator
doors opened, her sometimes-boyfriend was
sitting across from it. He had come to spend the
evening with her because he felt sorry for her.

Suddenly, the guilt of what she had done swept over her, and she began to cry.

Each time we tell a lie, we set a trap. Someone might find out. Most lies have the potential of hurting someone. We do not have the right to do anyone harm. God watches each of us to see whether we will commit ourselves to living lives of truth or not. When we choose correctly, He rejoices and blesses us richly.

I want to be an honest person, showing my love and respect for other people by my honesty. Help me to destroy that part of me which is prone to lie and deceive. Give me a portion of Your truth by which I might live. Amen.

Blessings and Curses

Faithful are the wounds of a friend;
but the kisses of an enemy are deceitful.

PROVERBS 27:6

Jesus waited in the garden. His disciples had
dozed off and He was alone to speak with
God. He prayed hard and long, and when He
finished, He looked up to see the approaching
torches of soldiers and magistrates. He awakened
His disciples, and to their amazement, one of their
own was leading the aggressors. Judas looked
upon Christ, and he felt icy. He moved forward to
embrace the Lord, then kissed Him on the cheek,
as if to say good-bye and that he was sorry. Jesus
pulled back and said through pain and anguish,
"A kiss? You come and you betray me with a kiss?"

Have you ever thought how painful that action
was to Christ? An act usually associated with love
was used to signal destruction. Someone that
Christ had trusted and befriended paid Him back
by turning Him over to the authorities, and he did
it with a kiss.

There are times when a friend will strike us in order to wake us up to danger or to bring us back to reality. Those blows are a blessing. But when someone hurts us under the pretense of love, that is the worst kind of pain. God wants us to deal with each other honestly. We cannot have things both ways. If we are not for God, we are against Him, and we should never compound our crime with hypocrisy.

Each time I sin, Father, I betray You with a kiss. I claim to love You, but then I do the things I know You hate. Please forgive me, Lord. Help me to be better, I pray. Amen.

Rejuvenation

Ointment and perfume rejoice the heart: so doth the
sweetness of a man's friend by hearty counsel.

Proverbs 27:9

The day had been so hot and tiring. All she could think of was soaking in a nice tub full of bubbles. It was the least she deserved.

She stepped into the warm, fragrant bath and immediately the tensions and heat of the day were banished. As she soaked, her muscles loosened and she relaxed. There was very little in life which was as nice as a good soak in a tub after a trying day. She felt like she could face anything the world would throw at her after her bath. It didn't take a whole lot, but she was refreshed and ready to meet life again.

A good conversation with a trusted friend can be every bit as refreshing as the aforementioned bath. There can be nothing quite so gratifying as

spending time with a good friend, just talking
things over. We need someone with whom we can
share secrets and dreams. That is why prayer is so
powerful. Anytime, anywhere, we can have a talk
with God, which will strengthen and renew us.
He can give us the strength to meet the world
head-on, and He will never leave us. He so wants
for us to come to Him to share our lives with
Him. It pleases Him to know that we love Him
enough to want to spend time with Him.

*I come to You knowing that You will not judge,
condemn, or mock. Thank You for being so close
whenever I need You. I could not want a better friend
in my life. I love You, Lord. Amen.*

CONSIDERATION

He that blesseth his friend with a loud voice, rising early
in the morning, it shall be counted a curse to him.

PROVERBS 27:14

It was not always easy being a night owl. Staying up late was only a pleasure when she was allowed to sleep in late. Since they had moved to the new neighborhood, she had met a few people, and they all arose around 6:00 a.m. That was fine if that's what they wanted to do. The problem was that they called her up after breakfast, which for them was 7:00. She knew that they were just trying to be friendly, but sometimes she wanted to scream at them. She had tried nicely to tell them that she liked sleeping in, but they still called by 8:00. She didn't know how long she would be able to tolerate their friendliness until it drove her completely crazy!

Consideration is an important Christian quality. If we love and respect other people, then we will want to know what is pleasing to them, and we will try to accommodate them. If we force ourselves on others, then we are being selfish. God doesn't want anyone to force their will on anyone else. Instead, He wants us to do for others everything in our power to make them comfortable and happy. To serve means to do what other people need and want. We do not get to set the rules, but we follow the rules of love set down by God.

Lord, I sometimes think I know what is desired of me, but I don't always ask. Help me to be sensitive to the needs of others, that I might serve them and bring them joy and comfort. Amen.

A REFLECTION OF CHRIST

As in water face answereth to face,
so the heart of man to man.

PROVERBS 27:19

It was nice to get away from the city to spend a day at the lake. The sky was crystal clear, and the bright sunshine felt wonderful. The trees were in full color, as the cool days came on. They walked along the lake, which was smooth as glass. The view across the lake was mirrored perfectly on its surface. The reflection caused the beauty of the

view to be doubled. The image on the lake was just slightly out of focus, and in places it rippled. The colors weren't quite as brilliant, but it was still exhilarating.

The image reflected from water is slightly imperfect and it is not as clear as the object it reflects. The same can be said of one's soul. It is merely a reflection of the soul of God in whose image it was created. As we grow closer to God, the image comes into sharper focus and it more closely resembles the soul of our Creator. The goal of Christians should be to become as much like God as is possible. It isn't complex, though that doesn't make it easy. All we have to do is let God finish the work He has begun in us. If we turn our lives over to God, then He will make us over in His image, and He will fill in the details which are lacking. He wants nothing more than for our souls to merge with His, so that both object and reflection are one.

Lord, I want to be one with You in soul, mind, and being. Help me to be the creation You want. I am alive to serve and to bless. Work through me that others may know Your great love and power. Amen.

COMPROMISING

Better is the poor that walketh in his uprightness,
than he that is perverse in his ways, though he be rich.

PROVERBS 28:6

It was the offer of a lifetime. He had the chance to invest in a project that was sure to make money. His brother brought the proposal to him to let him in on it. He was tempted, but there was a drawback. The project entailed driving some people from their homes in order to get some building done. There were some shady dealings

going on, and the people were being robbed by the company doing the building. None of the homeowners were even remotely aware of the value of their property. He thought long and hard about the offer, but he eventually decided against it. Anything which made him money at other people's expense wasn't worth the guilt. Better to stay poor and be able to look yourself in the eye in the mirror than to be rich and hate yourself for it.

Some things just aren't worth the compromise they entail. If we have to give up too much, then we find it harder and harder to live with ourselves. The poor person who feels good about himself is far richer than a wealthy person who lives with shame and guilt. God will bless the person who holds fast to values by granting peace and comfort.

Lord, I feel good that I have a chance to serve You. Help me never to compromise my values and beliefs. Let all of my actions reflect the love and devotion that I feel toward You. Amen.

THE POWER OF LOVE

As a roaring lion, and a ranging bear; so is a wicked
ruler over the poor people. The prince that
wanteth understanding is also a great oppressor: but he
that hateth covetousness shall prolong his days.

PROVERBS 28:15–16

The jungle was silent. The animals sensed the presence of their Lord. A thundering roar cut loose and sent the animals scurrying for cover. No animal dared confront the lion who ruled over the jungle land. His presence commanded respect and worship. However, it was a respect built on fear, not on love. As long as the beast had ruled, he had never known love. His subjects bowed to him, and they ran in fear, but he had never known what it meant to be well thought of.

Our Lord is a Lord of both power and love. It is well to fear the Lord, for He alone holds the power of true life and death. But we cannot have a relationship with anyone based on fear. There must be love, and our God makes it easy to love Him. He has given us a wonderful gift by giving us life, and He has proven His love for us by sending His only Son, our Lord Jesus Christ, to take the punishment for our sins so that we might one day be reunited with Him. Only a loving God gives so much to His children. We can rejoice that we do not serve a tyrant or a hateful master, but we serve the source of all that is good and right. His goodness shall endure forever, and we will be a part of it.

Thank You for not controlling me or forcing me to love You. I could not worship a God who made His children fear Him. Please help me to be the person You created me to be, so that I might return the love to You which You have given to me. Amen.

THE BEST GIFT

He that giveth unto the poor shall not lack:
but he that hideth his eyes shall have many a curse.

PROVERBS 28:27

There was a poor family who decided it was beyond their means to celebrate Christmas. They told their children not to expect presents, they planned a simple meal for Christmas day, they decided not to decorate, and they told the children the less said about Christmas the better. Some friends heard of the situation, and they pooled resources to give the family a Christmas they would never forget. On a day when the family went out, all the neighbors pitched in and decorated the house, putting up a tree and surrounding it with presents. The refrigerator was

stocked with wonderful treats and a feast fit for royalty. No indication was left of where the things had come from. When the family returned home they understood what Christmas was all about, and they truly did have a Christmas that none of them would ever forget.

It is important that we look for ways to give to those people who are in need. When we give unselfishly and totally, we begin to understand what God wants of us. God gave us the life of His Child Jesus, and it is when we give of ourselves to others that we please God the most. We can never pay God back for His great gift, but we should try whenever possible.

Show me ways that I can do good things for other people who are not as fortunate as I am. If nothing else, I can pray for them and give them my care and love. Help me to give what I can whenever I can. Amen.

THE GIFT OF LIFE

The bloodthirsty hate the upright:
but the just seek his soul.

PROVERBS 29:10

The headlines screamed of the atrocity.
A young woman had been killed while she
was home for the holidays. She had been assaulted
and beaten, and then killed. It was shocking any
time it happened, but there was something which
made it worse at holidays. The woman's family
would remember this every year when the season
rolled around, and it would place a cloud over
the celebrations.

The killer was caught just before Christmas,
and the parents of the girl wanted to see him.
They went into a room where a guard brought in
the accused. For a moment they sat looking at
each other; then the father said, "I don't know why
you killed our baby, and I don't really care. I want
to hate you, but I can't. God gave His Son so that
I might have life, and now I've given my daughter.
I hope that her life makes a difference. We came to
tell you that we're praying for you, and we hope

you really repent of what you have done. We won't stop praying until you're dead or saved." With that, the couple left.

How can we learn to love those who try to hurt us? Christ did it through the grace of God. God will supply us with the same power if only we will seek Him out.

Your gift to me in the life of Your Son is greater than I can comprehend. I want to know that love in my life. Help me to pray for the evil people in this world, that they might know the truth and love that You freely give. Amen.

BETTER TO LISTEN

Seest thou a man that is hasty in his words?
there is more hope of a fool than of him.

PROVERBS 29:20

The rush was on. The woman stood bewildered in the department store. Her husband had asked especially for a certain razor, and she was determined that she would get it for him. She finally got a sales clerk to wait on her, and she told him what she wanted. He looked at the counter, and then went into a fast sales pitch for a razor that was on sale. Five times she repeated what she wanted, and five times he tried to sell her something else. In frustration, she walked away to try another store.

Sometimes it feels like no one listens to us. We try to communicate what we mean, but it never gets through. It is frustrating when we deal with people who will not listen to what we say, and they themselves never quiet down. There is much to be said for the person who learns to listen instead of talk. When we listen, we learn. When we talk, we block learning. A fool loves to hear the sound of his own voice, but the wise person rejoices in what can be heard. We need to learn to listen, so that we can honestly help the people who come to us for our aid. If we talk, we will close people out and they will never come back. We deal foolishly, and we present an example that we cannot be proud of. God wants us to deal with people in love, and most people need to feel like they are being heard.

I know that You listen to me, Lord. Teach me to listen that I might be a blessing to those whom I serve. I want to learn all I can, and it is in silence that understanding comes. Amen.

A Godly Heritage

There is a generation that curseth their father,
and doth not bless their mother. There is a generation
that are pure in their own eyes, and yet is
not washed from their filthiness. There is a generation,
O how lofty are their eyes! and their eyelids
are lifted up. There is a generation, whose teeth are
as swords, and their jaw teeth as knives,
to devour the poor from off the earth,
and the needy from among men.

PROVERBS 30:11–14

His parents were such an embarrassment to him. They were old world Italians, and they just didn't fit in with his image. He had worked all his life to beat the stereotypes, and he'd done his best to deny his heritage. He lived in fear that his parents would show up at the wrong time and spoil everything. He was rich and popular, and he was ashamed of being associated with his garlic-eating parents.

There is nothing more sad than a person who rejects who he is and where he comes from. When we get so proud that we deny our families, then we have very little character or compassion. We should be proud of where we come from. Whether we are Italian, American, Russian, black, white, Christian, Jew, or any of a thousand other categories, we come from a single source, and that is God in heaven. We should be proud of that heritage. If we are proud of our heavenly Father, He will be proud of us, and we will know a happiness that will never, ever end. We are made holy through the love of God.

I am proud of You, Lord. How could I be otherwise? Without You nothing which now is could ever be. You have created everything, and You have made me special and unique. I am Your child, and I will love You forever. Amen.

God's Amazing Love

There be three things which are too wonderful
for me, yea, four which I know not: the way of an eagle
in the air; the way of a serpent upon a rock;
the way of a ship in the midst
of the sea; and the way of a man with a maid.

PROVERBS 30:18–19

The sky was lit up by a million pinpoints of light. The wonder of it all was too much. It was hard to imagine that a star once shone brighter than all the rest, which led people to a stable in Bethlehem. There a Babe was born who changed history. Standing outside looking up at all the stars made you know that there was indeed a God, and that He was good. The world was full of wonders which attested to His greatness: all the different creatures of the sea, the beauty of a ship on the ocean, the deep wonder of love. All of these things seemed magical, and indeed, they were.

They were full of a magic, which was God. His handiworks were testimony of His beauty and might.

And yet, more wonderful still was the knowledge that amidst all of this beauty and power, God had really one desire, and that was to love and be loved by me. How could that be? He had so much. He *is* so much. At times, I feel very insignificant and small, but then I think of God's great love, and I realize that I am somebody special, for I am the Lord's.

How can I thank You for what You have done for me? How can I thank You for all I have been given? How can I ever hope to be worthy of Your love? All I can do is praise You, love You, and give You my life. Amen.

FOOLISH CONSEQUENCES

If thou hast done foolishly in lifting up thyself,
or if thou hast thought evil, lay thine hand upon thy
mouth. Surely the churning of milk bringeth forth butter,
and the wringing of the nose bringeth forth blood:
so the forcing of wrath bringeth forth strife.

PROVERBS 30:32—33

For every action, there is an equal and opposite reaction. When we do something wrong, we can expect that we will have to suffer for it. Every day, the little boy had stopped to throw

stones at the birds, which roosted along the fence. He had never been much of a shot, and they always flew away before he could come close. One day, he hefted a rather large stone, and let it fly at the unsuspecting birds. The rock flew straight, and hit a bird, knocking it from the fence. In shock and horror, the boy raced up to the fence and picked up the lifeless bird. He began crying, telling the bird he hadn't meant to hurt it. He felt sick inside and helpless as he looked at his own handiwork.

Why is it that people tempt fate, and then they are so shocked when something goes wrong? If we play with fire, we will eventually get burned. If you strike someone hard enough on the nose, it will bleed. If you churn milk long enough, it will turn to butter. If you dwell in wrong and sinful acts, then you will have to encounter the wrath of God. It is not speculation, it is reality, and the wise understand this and do everything they can to avert the disaster which must result.

O Lord, help me to keep from living so foolishly. I act as if I am immortal, without doing the things which are required of me. I have much to learn, and only You can teach me. Please do so, Lord, I pray. Amen.

A Life of Blessing

*Who can find a virtuous woman? for her price
is far above rubies. The heart of her husband doth safely
trust in her, so that he shall have no need of spoil.
She will do him good and not evil all the days of her life.*

Proverbs 31:10–12

The trip was so long and hard. The burro kept staggering from side to side, and Mary felt as if she were going to burst. She and Joseph knew that the baby was coming soon, and they were trying desperately to find a place to rest. She never said a word of complaint. She knew that her child

was to be blessed, and she trusted in God that He would protect and shelter them. She did not know why she had been selected of all women to bring God's Son into the world, but she was filled with pride and excitement.

Joseph looked upon her and he felt glad. He was proud of Mary, and he felt doubly blessed by the Lord. He was entrusted to bring up the Son of the Most High God and to care for his own lovely wife. The pair moved on to Bethlehem joyful and at peace, for they knew that God was with them.

God is with us each day. When we live our lives according to His will, then we become a blessing to those around us. Wives become blessings to husbands, and husbands to wives, children to parents, and sisters to brothers. A life well lived is a gift, not only to God and ourselves, but to everyone we meet.

Make my life virtuous and good. Help me to bless the lives of my family and friends. Shine Your love through my life, that I may be a beacon of Your light. Help me to glorify You in all things. Amen.

PRECIOUS LOVE

She is not afraid of the snow for her household:
for all her household are clothed with scarlet.

PROVERBS 31:21

She looked back over her life, and she was
satisfied. Never once had they been rich.
Never once did they have more than they knew
what to do with. That didn't mean they'd ever been
poor. Her children had always had clothes to wear
and shoes for their feet and food enough to satisfy
their bellies. They had all had to pitch in to
make things go, but families ought to do that.
Her children loved each other. Other families got
tied up with gadgets and things, but hers had spent
their time in love and sharing. The family would
spend long hours talking and sitting around the
fire. Those were the good times. Those memories
were more precious than gold.

We can provide our family and friends with
many things, but we have nothing greater to give
than our love. If we will deal with people in love

and kindness, we give them something worth more than the finest possessions. Money can't compare with a great love that carries through our lives. God gives us such love. We may think that we are poor, that we don't have all the things we want, but if we have His love then we are richer than kings and queens. Nothing compares with the love of God, and the person who knows such love will never know want.

Father, I adore You. You have been so good to me and have shared so much. Help me to share what You have given to me with others. Let me share the treasure that is in my heart. Amen.

WELL DONE

She looketh well to the ways of her household,
and eateth not the bread of idleness. Her children arise
up, and call her blessed; her husband also,
and he praiseth her. Many daughters have done
virtuously, but thou excellest them all.

PROVERBS 31:27–29

Emma sat encircled by friends and family, and she was at peace. Looking around at her family, she felt that God was pleased with her. Her sons and daughters, grandsons and granddaughters, great-grandsons and great-granddaughters were all fine people who knew what it meant to love and what it meant to have faith. Her family had been brought up in the fear of the Lord, and it was worth it. In a world which was full of hurt and fear, her family was full of

hope and love. There was a crowd of people here to celebrate with her, but most importantly she knew, God was here, too. She looked forward to meeting Him face-to-face.

When we have lived well, we can stand before God unashamed. He will look upon us, and the radiance of His face will warm and comfort us. He will tell us that we have run the race well, and that we have been good and faithful servants, and all the hurts, frustrations, and disappointments of this life will fade away to nothingness. In our meeting with our Maker, we will understand fully just how wonderful the gift of life really is.

I look at the beauty and wonder in this world, and something deep inside tells me that I haven't seen anything yet. I look at the evil and pain in the world, and something cries out inside that I don't belong here. Be with me all of my days, Lord, and bring me at last to Your eternal glory, I pray. Amen.

Dan and Nancy Dick are a husband-wife writing team who make their home in Tennessee. They have coauthored *Daily Wisdom from the Bible* as well as the best-selling *Devotions for Dieters*.

Scripture Index

Proverbs